The Resilience Advantage

The Resilience Advantage

Stop Managing Stress and Find Your Resilience

Richard S. Citrin, PhD, MBA
Alan Weiss, PhD

 BUSINESS EXPERT PRESS

The Resilience Advantage: Stop Managing Stress and Find Your Resilience

Copyright © Business Expert Press, LLC, 2016

First published in 2016 by
Business Expert Press, LLC
222 East 46th Street, New York, NY 10017
www.businessexpertpress.com

ISBN-13: 978-1-63157-373-6 (paperback)
ISBN-13: 978-1-63157-374-3 (e-book)

Business Expert Press Human Resource Management
and Organizational Behavior Collection

Collection ISSN: 1946-5637 (print)
Collection ISSN: 1946-5645 (electronic)

Cover and interior design by S4Carlisle Publishing Services
Private Ltd., Chennai, India

First edition: 2016

10 9 8 7 6 5 4 3 2 1

Printed in the United States of America.

Dedication

To Susan, the American Airlines flight attendant, who, shortly after 9/11, demonstrated to me what resilience is all about.
To my two adult children, Corinne and Ken, who walked the path of resilience before I had a name for it.

Richard Citrin

For my granddaughters, Alaina and Gabrielle.

Alan Weiss

Advanced Quotes For
The Resilience Advantage

"*The Resilience Advantage* is a practical guide to navigating a world seemingly gone mad with its addiction to busyness and stress. In clear and accessible language, Richard Citrin and Alan Weiss show us how to see past the frenzy and panic of our complicated daily lives and dip into the deep reservoir of calm adaptability that exists within each of us. This book reminds us how capable and strong we really are, no matter how down or challenged we may sometimes feel. It is a powerful and empowering read that offers its readers mastery over the only thing we ever truly control: the attitude with which we embrace our own lives."

Grant Oliphant
President, The Heinz Endowments

"Citrin and Weiss, using their decades of insightful experience working with both individuals and organizations in stressful and even devastating circumstances, have created an understandable and actionable blueprint to increase resiliency. 'Plan, navigate, recover and strengthen.' This formula for *The Resilience Advantage* provides both insight and actionable ways to improve enjoyment and achievement."

Michael Parkinson, MD, MPH, FACPM
Past President, American College of Preventive Medicine

"Richard and Alan challenge us to reframe our relationship with stress in a positive way. With resilience as our partner, you show how we can embrace stress to enhance our performance both professionally and personally."

Cabot Earle
CEO, Microbac Laboratories, Inc.

"*The Resilience Advantage* is packed with practical techniques for turning life's unavoidable stresses into power packs that propel you forward in the areas you care most deeply about. Whether it's rebuilding a relationship, achieving a significant career goal, or upping your performance to play your best, this book has tactics and strategies that will help you get better results in every area of life."

Seth Kahan
Author of Getting Change Right
and Getting Innovation Right

"*The Resilience Advantage* provides a roadmap for employees and business leaders alike to turn stress and adversity to their advantage. The book changes the conversation around stress in our workplaces and in our lives away from the notion of "managing stress," to instead look at our inherent capacity for being resilient. It offers practical advice on how to use the resilience principles to address workplace and personal challenges. This book has great application for workplace health and well being and will help corporate leaders lead the way to a healthier and more productive workplace."

Alberto Colombi, MD, MPH
Former Global Medical Director, PPG Industries

"Think you know something about resilience? Think again.

Much like the martial art of Aikido, which uses the energy of the opponent to your benefit, so too, does Richard Citrin use the energy of a setback to help you bounce back faster and stronger than ever. Citing both the existing psychological literature and building on his own work,

Richard Citrin has a new and unique view of resilience that no working professional should be without.

Providing new thinking on what were once thought well-worn trails, Citrin gives pragmatic, how-to advice to immediately improve your resiliency. Here you'll learn how to deal with the contract that falls through, the promotion not obtained, and even the negative thinking which often follows success.

Grab this book, find a comfortable spot, and let Richard Citrin and Alan Weiss guide you to a world where every day you can be smarter, stronger and faster because you have *The Resilience Advantage*."

Mark Rodgers
Consultant and Award Winning Author
of The Persuasion Equation

"The management and self-help bookshelves are overflowing with volumes teaching so-called stress management techniques. So why are we are more stressed out than ever? *The Resilience Advantage* reframes stress as a natural, necessary, and even beneficial component of modern life. More important, it offers readers specific, practical tools to build on their own strengths and become more resilient in the process. It's a much-needed and welcome contribution, filling an important gap in the literature. These methods work—I use many of them with my clients every day."

Emerson M. Wickwire, PhD, ABPP, CBSM
Director, Insomnia Program,
University of Maryland School of Medicine

"Gain a rare insider's perspective on understanding your innate capacity to effectively embrace your daily life and work stresses, rather than just manage them. You'll also receive a roadmap for developing your responses to any situation with the goal of optimizing your life and those of your family and colleagues. Take a deep breath and change your life."

Donald Machan, MD, DDS, JD, MBA
Retired Judge and Health Care Consultant

"Rarely do thought leaders like Citrin and Weiss come along with insights profound enough to completely upend a staid topic like stress management and truly pioneer a new paradigm. *The Resilience Advantage* offers provocation and practical support to companies and individuals seeking to promote stress resilience and create healthier, happier, and more productive ways of living and working. A must-read."

Kristy Trautman
Executive director, FISA Foundation

"In a crowded, chaotic world, it's a given that sooner or later we will encounter significant challenges. How we respond and the mindset we take determine whether stress rules us or we maintain control. In this book, Richard Citrin and Alan Weiss present us with a fresh approach to the fine art of building resilience, and offer helpful suggestions for applications in personal and professional situations."

Linda J. Popky
Author of Marketing Above the Noise:
Achieve Strategic Advantage
with Marketing That Matters

Abstract

For 70 years, psychologists, wellness experts, and physicians have been teaching people that they can manage the stress in their lives.

They have been wrong.

Over the past 15 years, there has been a revolution in how business, communities, and governments around the globe address challenge and adversity. Their goal has shifted from trying to manage these events to instead recognizing that we have to build resilient systems that help us prepare for them, navigate through them in real time, and bounce back— or better still, bounce forward. The resilience movement admits the fact that we can't always keep bad things from happening and that we must develop strategies that help us learn from the challenges, not be victimized by them.

The Resilience Advantage takes these ideas and those from neuropsychology, education, the arts, sports, and positive psychology and puts them into practical and effective strategies for individuals and organizations who struggle with the day–to-day stresses of today's complex and challenging workplace.

Despite our efforts to help people manage their stress, this model is fatally flawed. To work towards resilience, however, with its understanding and acceptance that challenges are inherent and perhaps should be even welcomed, relieves us of the pressures associated with trying to man- age our stress.

The Resilience Advantage will transform how you think about stress and help you to move from being a stress victim to being a stress victor.

Keywords

Stress management, stress resilience, business resilience, resilience, burnout, positive psychology, stress, workplace challenges, stress management training, risk management, health and wellness

Table of Contents

Acknowledgments

Numerous professional colleagues have shared with me their insights about the science of resilience and the art of business. Particular among them are Alberto Colombi and Ken Schaper formerly from PPG Industries, Michael Parkinson, Sherry Neubert from Goodyear Tire and Rubber, and Matt Steenson, Lakhbir Lamba, and Tom Kunz from PNC Bank and Stephanie Doliveira from Sheetz.

My business-consulting community has kept me on the business straight and narrow, including Hugh Blane, Judy Chan, Mark Rodgers, Roberta Matuson, Linda Popky, Chad Barr, and Vanessa Heckman. I am especially fortunate to have such an amazing business colleague as Michael Couch. My coauthor, Alan Weiss, changed my thinking about business six years ago and about writing six months ago. Cynthia Winton-Henry and Phil Porter, founders of Interplay, have helped me discover the artful side of myself. Discussions I've had with good friends like Kristy Trautman, Aradhna Oliphant, Pam Meadowcroft, Steve Siegel, and Randall King were especially helpful throughout this project. Clients and colleagues at PPG Industries, American Airlines, The Software Engineering Institute at CMU, The University of Pittsburgh Medical Center, Sheetz, Goodyear Tire and Rubber, PNC Bank, and Leadership Pittsburgh have shown me different aspects of how organizations work to address resilience in their workplace.

I'm blessed to have such an amazing family. My parents, Pearl and Jack, would be most proud of this effort, while my brothers, Chuck and Jay, have been my best supporters from day one. My children, Corinne, Kevin, and Ken, have taught me much about being a grownup. My wonderful wife, Sheila, has been the spirit and face of resilience in my life for our 40 years together.

Thank you all.

Richard Citrin

Introduction

Resilience has been a hot topic for the past 15 years within business and society, but the real question is whether the topic and the ideas it promulgates actually change people, businesses, communities, and even global systems. Can learning about resilience cause us to shift our thinking and behavior as we address challenges and adverse situations that occur in the workplace, in our lives, and in the larger culture?

For resilience to go beyond being just a hot topic for discussion, the ideas of resilience need to resonate with people. The principles of resilience need to prove effective as we deal with challenging, difficult, and even adverse situations and the practices of resilience need to be accessible and easy to implement.

If you find yourself overwhelmed at work, exhausted at the end of the day, and not having the physical or mental energy to enjoy your work and your family, then you will find the ideas in this book helpful. This book is for anyone who feels that they are not able to address their stress as effectively as they would like to be able to do. And in my conversations, that seems like a lot of people.

We take a different approach to resilience for individuals and organizations. For us, resilience is more than just bounce back. We define the resilience advantage as,

Our ability to effectively plan for, navigate successfully, and gracefully recover from challenging and stressful events in such a way that we are strengthened by the experience.

This book will change the way you and your organization think about and address the kinds of workplace problems that cause everyone to feel overwhelmed, frustrated, and, at the end of the day, defeated. Instead, you will find that our approach to resilience, while not taking away your stress, will provide you with a new perspective and pragmatic tools to help you take back your power over stress.

We have divided this book into three sections. In Part 1, we discuss our culture's current relationship with the stress management model, why this approach has failed us, and how we can use a resilience model to have stress work *for* us rather than against us.

In Part 2, we introduce the Resilience Continuum, which includes ways to address stress *before* it comes our way, how we can navigate in real time through the challenges gracefully, and finally ways to bounce back from stressful situations stronger and in a way in which we learn from those events, so that we do more than just bounce back but bounce forward.

Part 3 looks at specific ways to put resilience into play for yourself in your workplace. The workplace chapter provides ideas on how leaders can use resilience thinking to transform their workplace, so that low-hanging stress inducers, like poorly run meetings and a lack of recognition, can be eliminated. More challenging strategies, such as workload management and building high-performing teams, as a way of mitigating stress before it happens are also discussed.

We also provide additional resources at our website, ***www.theresilienceadvantage.com***. In this site you will find templates for building a resilience plan, podcasts and audio tapes for mindfulness, organizational activities for building resilience, as well as tips for individuals, managers, and leaders on creating a resilient life and workplace. You can use the password **resilienceadvantage** to access the materials.

Even though it seems that the normal state of our life is to be stressed out and burned up, this is not the case. We are truly hardwired to handle our stress in a way in which we are successful in how we deal with it and what we can learn from it. That is our resilience advantage.

PART 1

Time for a Change

I've always been a fan of history, as I know we can learn much from the past. Yet, what is important about history is that we use it to learn new ways to thrive in our time.

When it comes to our approach to addressing life's challenges and its subsequent stress, people have always developed ways to help us cope. The Greek philosopher Epictetus believed that the key to overcoming hardships and adversity was to develop an approach that distinguished between those things within our control and those that were not. In ancient Roman days, mothers intentionally limited their emotional bonding with newborn children until they passed the critical one- or two-month period that would assure the child's likely survival. William Shakespeare provided many views of how to deal with stress in Elizabethan England. In Hamlet, Polonius advises his son Laertes on how to avoid disappointments and secure a successful life.

In our first chapter, we'll discuss the current model that our culture defines as the best approach to addressing life's adversities. We call this the stress management model, and its 70-year history has directed how we approach our life's trials. We'll show you why the model is flawed and how it has failed us miserably.

In Chapter 2, we discuss how the stress management model has actually created the perception that we don't handle stress very well, which then creates more stress for us. We worry about how badly we are stressed and strive to do anything we can to avoid stress! We go on to discuss new ways to think about how stress works for us in our lives, and how a global movement toward resilience can be applied to each of us at home and at work.

We conclude Part 1 with ideas about how we each can begin applying the idea of resilience to change our thinking about the daily travails in our life. We introduce a new and expanded definition of resilience that sets the stage for a whole set of tools we can use to our advantage.

CHAPTER 1

Sorry for the Mistake: Why 70 Years of Stress Management Training Has Left Us Stressed

Ideas about managing stress began in the 1950s when we first started learning about the physiological implication of stress on our health and well-being. The message we received then was that stress was bad for us and that we wanted to avoid it as much as possible. If we could not avoid it, then we should try to manage it as best as we can.

Survey after survey has shown, however, that everyone's stress level is higher and higher than it was before. That can only lead to at least one conclusion which is that the approaches we are using to address challenges and stress in our lives are not working. Furthermore, we want to do more than just survive our existence. We want our lives to be satisfying, rewarding, and amazing, too.

So a new approach to thinking about and addressing life challenges needs to be put in place. It's time to stop thinking that we can actually manage stress and instead take the radical step to seek out a new approach to addressing life challenges—by being resilient in the face of stressful challenges and life adversities.

You Don't Manage Stress; Stress Manages You

I remember a time I offered a stress management presentation to a group of third-year medical students who were already well under way in their practicum assignments at the University Medical Center. I had done scores of stress management programs as part of my professional career. I was told that these students worked long shifts and had significant classroom assignments, and that their professor was a real bear of a teacher who expected nothing short of perfection from these aspiring physicians.

I came to the presentation with a plethora of handouts and slides to share with them about how stress worked and how they could successfully manage their stress. I proceeded to talk to them about getting enough sleep, eating well, and learning different approaches to mental and physical rest. As I often did, I conducted a breathing exercise with the students where I had them close their eyes and engage in mental relaxation. Pretty soon, I started to hear one student snore, then another, and then a third. After a few minutes, the rest of the students had their calmness wrecked by the sound of their colleagues sawing logs and a light laughter began to fill the classroom. After a bit of physical shaking to wake up the sleepy heads, everyone was soon ready to talk about the experience.

The students told me that they thought it was impossible to manage stress in their environment and perhaps in other workplace environments. Long hours, mental and physical demands that limited rest, and expectations for performance that went beyond anything they had ever endured meant that they could not take any time to think about resting or relaxing or managing their stress in any way. They just had to hold on for their dear lives, do the best they could, and plan for collapse sometime after the semester was over.

I walked away from the presentation thinking I was glad that I wasn't in medical school but convinced that there had to be some way to help them and others find a way to successfully manage stress. For several years, I persisted on this journey to help people and organizations **manage** stress effectively.

Unfortunately, I was wrong and those medical students were right. What has become clear to me over the past several years is that we really can't manage stress. The messages, training, and information we've received about "stress management" have actually led us to be more stressed than ever. The challenge, it seems, is that the more and more we try to manage our stress, the less successful we are in doing so. This actually creates *more* stress as now we have the added burden of feeling like failures at being able to manage factors such as time, rest, workload, and family responsibilities in a comfortable manner.

It seems ironic that while we know more and more about stress than ever before, we feel less and less capable of dealing with our stress, as is reported in survey after survey.

It's been over 70 years since the idea of stress management was first introduced to us. It derived from scientific research that revealed how our biological bodies respond to most events that create change in our system. When an unexpected event occurs, which may be good or bad such as having your Friday afternoon business trip plane ride home cancelled or your soccer-playing son lose the championship game our body reacts to those events in a way that releases stress hormones. These hormones help us cope with such events effectively. They may help by sharpening focus so that we can immediately jump on the airlines' website to find an alternative route home, or it may provide us with a bit more empathy so that we can help turn our son's disappointment into resolve for next season. These reactions are "hardwired" and the response of our bodies is automatic.

It's this biological response or imperative that makes managing stress so impossible. Our bodies and minds are going to react to stressful situations in a specific way, and our pitiful efforts to try to manage this are going to fall well short of making a significant difference in our lives. We cannot prevent that, and might as well come to terms with that inability.

The truth of the matter is that stress manages *us* much more effectively than we manage *it*. Consider for a moment how you experience these stressful situations:

- Your boss walks into your office and tells you that she has some good news for you. The company is starting a new division and they want you to head it up. It'll mean a promotion in title, increase in compensation, and a new team to lead. When she walks out of your office, you literally jump with joy and dance around before calling your spouse to announce, with great pride, your fantastic news. After you hang up, you begin to get a tight feeling in your stomach about your new responsibility.
- You're driving down the highway, enjoying the view, when a piece of tire explodes from a semi up ahead. You immediately

slam on your brakes to gain a bit of time to figure out what to do and manage to veer your way around the imposing piece of rubber coming your way. Afterward, you notice your heart is racing, your hands are sweating, and you take a deep breath to gain what feels like a little sense of control.

- Your grown daughter calls home to announce that you are going to be a grandparent for the first time. You feel like your heart is going to burst with joy. She's describing all the details about her meeting with her doctor, but all you can see is your baby girl who is now herself going to have her own little baby. Tears well up in your eyes and you start praying that her pregnancy and the baby will be healthy.

Although these events are different in nature in fact some are positive while others are negative and still others are both our physical, emotional, and mental reactions are very similar. We have some kind of somatic reaction to the stressful event such as a racing heart, a change in our breathing, and thoughts that propel us to find safety or celebrate success. We can't help but be excited and hopeful about the promotion and grandbaby, and can't be anything other than nervous and fearful about a piece of tire tread traveling 70 miles an hour heading our way on the highway.

The current thinking about stress management is not much different from what it was when we first realized that stress plays such a critical and dramatic part of our lives. If you look for tips about managing stress from your physician, your personal trainer, or just Google "stress management," what you will hear is that you "should try to relax," or "take some deep breaths." The list of stress management techniques is actually pages long, and although any one of them and even many of them may be

We can use stress to influence because of these immediate, uncontrollable reactions that strike like lightning. Remember the old story of a woman who calls home from college to tell her parents she's pregnant, the man involved with her was arrested for drugs, and he took all her money? Then she says to her speechless, stunned parents, "Hey, I'm just kidding, but I did flunk chemistry."

helpful in dealing with stressful situations, they do not really address the key issue of how we come to terms with the idea that stress is a natural, healthy, and actually helpful aspect to our lives, and that we need a new approach and new way of understanding how we can genuinely embrace the stress in our lives so that we can see its gifts.

"Hang in There, Baby"

The poster has been around as long as the stress management model has been perpetrating its perspective that we can manage stress. The kitten is holding onto a rope, looking down and fearing the outcome if she lets go. The message is clear: In today's terrifying world, sometimes all we can do is hold on for dear life and hope that whatever is waiting to cause us harm will move away, so that we can just get on with our existence.

In addition to the ridiculous notion that we can actually manage stress, the second great failure of the stress management model is the idea that we are victims of our stress and that even if we try to control or manage our stress, we won't, in reality, be very effective in doing so. It's as if our day-to-day existence as well as our life destiny is outside our control and we are merely targets of whatever our life environment brings to us.

This notion is subtle in how it operates in our life, but we can hear it in the words and phrases we use. Terms such as "I'm so stressed out," "I'm out of control," or "I can't handle this" reflect the notion that we are somehow unable to deal with the daily fluctuations of our lives.

Growing up in my generation meant that I would spend my time out of the house, hanging out with friends and exploring our world, playing ball, and climbing rocks. Inevitably, those actions would lead to cuts or bruises, having disagreements, or even fights with friends. Learning how to make do by ourselves without any supervision or protection from our parents meant we had to face up to our own stress.

According to an article written by Hanna Rosin in 2014 in *The Atlantic* entitled "The Overprotected Kid,"[i] all that changed in 1978 when a child playing on a tall slide in a Chicago playground fell from the top of the slide and hit his head on the asphalt pavement causing permanent brain and physical damage. Subsequent lawsuits and settlements meant the end of these play areas as we know them, an apparent belief by parents that the world is an incredibly dangerous place to be, and that kids are not safe being off by themselves.

We used to run through traffic and play ball on the streets, and jump over steel cyclone fences, and none of us was ever badly injured. But now, playgrounds designed for safe play ushered in a new era of perceived danger all around. Lawsuits, of course, never help.

This message has expanded not just to playgrounds but also to many other aspects of family life so that today, kids don't walk to school by themselves, they go only on supervised play dates with friends, and their time is scheduled from morning to night. Pretty soon, kids will probably be wearing body cameras to track their daily activities. We already use cameras in their rooms.

We'll be living in the world of *The Truman Show*.

The good news about this phenomenon is that despite the busyness of adults' everyday life, parents are actually spending more time with their children than they were a generation ago. Moms and dads are with their kids after school and on weekends at athletic games, recitals, and other events and know more about their kids than ever before. The downside is that kids have few opportunities to explore the world on their own since parents want to protect their children from stressful events and ensure that they are in structured, supervised activities only. *Kids miss out on developing their own abilities to cope with everyday normal challenges that prepare them for adulthood.*

Furthermore, this loss of freedom to explore the world and to make kids encounter the world on their own leads to children who are less energetic, talkative, humorous, and imaginative, according to research cited by Rosin in her *Atlantic* article.[ii]

We pay a price for protecting our kids and ourselves from experiencing the world and its associated stressors. Learning to cope and even succeed with complex challenges effectively means that we build more confidence in our ability to take on the world. Kids pay the price by not having enough diverse experiences by the time they reach adulthood. Businesses pay the price in lost innovation, less prudent risk, lower creativity, and reduced energy.

Not surprisingly, this quality of caution and fear of facing stress can be seen in workplace dynamics. Employees are afraid to take action because it might upset the apple cart. They sit in meetings waiting for the boss to speak up and state a position before they express their ideas. They might have a great idea but tend to discount it because they don't feel as if their opinion will be respected or that it will be criticized away. Events that will increase stress levels prompt a feeling of just hanging on for dear life.

Case Study: The Poor Performing Team

Recently, I was brought in to work with a group of sales executives who were all capable in their own professional areas, but when I interviewed them to determine how well they all worked as a team, they gave themselves a unanimous "D" in their performance. There were numerous problems facing the team, including a lack of clarity of mission and roles, ineffective connections with other parts of the organization, a leader who was busy with corporate activities and did not fully participate with the group, and a lack of basic resources with which to get their work done.

Far and away, however, the unspoken truth about the team's lack of success was related to poor communication and no trust among members. In my interviews with the staff, I saw a group of professionals committed to what they were told to achieve but so emotionally wounded that during my interviews, some of them turned red-faced with anger, while others were shame-faced with tears. They were a passionate but unhappy group.

There did not seem to be a way for them to express their frustrations and disappointments and, as a result, they began to feel powerless in their roles. Several of them told me there was nothing they could do about their situation, that they were just stuck in their jobs (maybe forever), and could not see a way out of the situation. One person even told me that she just had to find a way to "hang in there" until things got better. She had no idea how that would happen, however.

She along with her colleagues had succumbed to the idea that they had no control over their workplace stress and challenges and

continued

concluded that they were inevitably locked into a situation from which there was no exit. Although no one said to me, "I feel so stressed and powerless in this situation and don't believe I can do anything about it," it seemed clear to me that was her key message.

We talked for a few minutes about ideas and options that she could consider. We played out a number of different scenarios and what would happen if she decided to take more charge of her situation, giving in to her sense of futility and powerlessness. Soon, her spirit rose a bit as she saw that there were options and possibilities to what seemed like an impossible situation. She began to move from a state of victimization to a state of power in just a few minutes. She was showing her resilience by confronting her challenges and not running away from them.

Our world has become so complex and overwhelming that we often feel as if it is impossible to have any sense of control. The tools we have learned to deal with these challenges as presented in stress management models tell us that we actually can't do very much more than "hang in there, baby." There is more than hanging on and instead we have to put ourselves "out there" to experience the world fully and fearlessly.

Recently, I saw a Facebook video a friend of mine had posted showing her six-year-old daughter getting ready for her first solo, two-wheeled bicycle ride. Her partner had not wanted their daughter to try out training wheels but instead wanted her to go from tricycle to two wheels straight away. As has been happening for several generations now, there was the video of Susan running alongside her daughter Meg's bike, arms extended and ready to grab onto the seat of the bike in case her daughter started to wobble. Meg is a pretty good little athlete and soon she was on her way around the schoolyard navigating her way around and showing off to her proud parents and the Facebook universe how independent she could be on her bike.

Hopefully, she'll have some stumbles and tumbles and will probably fall and scrape her knees and probably her pride. She may very well cry, but I bet she'll soon be back up on her bike. We need to allow our kids to fall and fail and recover, so that they can grow into adults who can fall and fail and be resilient.

We Don't Want to Just Hang on, We Want to Thrive

The current stress management model actually keeps us from being happy. Consider how much energy is consumed every day by our regrets, bemoaning, catastrophizing, and plain old worrying about the stressors we can't control. These small and large disappointments consume our thoughts and focus and tend to accrete, like stalagmites in our minds. They often lead to bad days. All because we believe we have control over things for which we actually do *not*.

When a stressful situation occurs, our body responds in one of three ways:

- We want to do battle with the stress—*the fight reaction*
- We want to run from the stress—*the flight reaction*
- We want to lay low and hope it will pass—*the freeze reaction*

These responses to stress are our biological way of coping with challenging events. They simply are how we are programmed to respond. Instead of accepting that they occur and recognizing that they are our biological response, we take them to be negative occurrences and create a whole world around how stressed we are in our lives. I call this the "double dump," which means that we feel bad about something negative and then make it worse by blaming ourselves for making our lives so unbearable.

This is not how we want to live our lives. We want to live our lives by acknowledging that we are very blessed and lucky to be living in such amazing times and with people who love us.

How can we begin to shift the focus from "yuck to yum?"

Thomas Jefferson wrote about the "pursuit of happiness" in the Declaration of Independence and, for most of us, it is a goal to which we aspire. We may get close to it but never really get there, and if we think we get there, it is only for a fleeting moment.

Jefferson never defined exactly what he meant by the pursuit of happiness, but today's researchers have identified ideas about what happiness means. The best part of their ideas is that each of us gets to define exactly what makes us happy. The term subjective well-being (SWB) has been used to give each of us the ability to examine our own overall life situation and decide if that is happiness for us. In the simplest sense, happiness can be having many more positive emotions than negative emotions. Dan Gilbert's work at Harvard on "synthetic happiness" is another aspect.[iii] "Being fired was the best thing that ever happened to me" isn't a shallow rationalization, for example, but a true exercise in defining our own happiness.

We can think of happiness as having two key aspects. The first is related to the attainment of long-term goals. As we get older we put together strings of events that lead to goal attainment and success. We complete college, get married, start a family, help our kids grow in a healthy way, and maybe get that sports car we always dreamed of driving. At work, we do well, get promoted, are recognized, receive raises, obtain more power. Based on these longer-term life and business goals, when we get a win, we feel good about the world and ourselves. We've overcome whatever stress or challenge we faced and we get to celebrate and enjoy it.

A second way to experience happiness is by simply smelling the roses every day. Researchers define this approach as moment-by-moment joy, and this is the gift that keeps on giving. Think about all the cool things that happen every day. Your kids give you a hug, your favorite lilac bush is blooming and its fragrance wafts up toward your deck, your boss thanks you for helping out with a project that brought in some new business. Each of these singular events can be viewed as a positive occurrence, and our attention to these small pleasures creates positive feelings.

These definitions of happiness might be called natural happiness, as defined by Gilbert. He defines *natural happiness* as "what we get (happiness) when we get what we wanted." Gilbert also talks about *synthetic happiness* as "what we make when we don't get what we wanted."[iv]

According to Gilbert's research, synthetic happiness yields the same level of pleasure and satisfaction as natural happiness, but with synthetic happiness, we get to decide that we'll feel good and positive about the events that happen for us. It's the classic case of making lemonade out of lemons. And when you put natural happiness together with synthetic happiness, you have a great combination for living fully and thriving completely.

How do you rate your happiness? On the spider chart in Figure 1.1, we've listed 10 areas of life that you can rate in terms of your happiness level from 1–10.

Rate your overall happiness in each area and then connect the dots to see where you are experiencing more joy and where you are experiencing less. Of course, feel free to substitute any areas of your life that you want to include in your happiness chart. Since many of these life issues are subjected to the stressors of daily life, you'll be able to go back and assess your own progress in finding more joy as you begin to see that the challenges of these life issues do not have to overwhelm and stress you out.

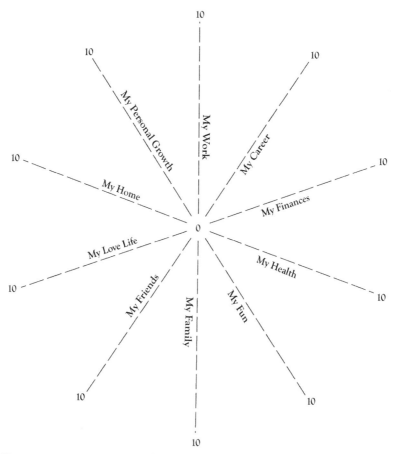

Figure 1.1 Spider Chart of Happiness

Now, let's examine your moment-to-moment happiness (Figure 1.2). Thinking of the last 24 hours, jot down on the lines below five things that happened that brought you a sense of happiness and rate them from 1 to 10 on how pleasurable they were for you. It could have been a commercial that was funny on TV or a Facebook post that touched your heart. Perhaps you had coffee with a colleague at work and he thanked you for helping out on a project, or your daughter texted you about getting an A on her math exam.

Later in this book, we'll be discussing the negativity bias, which is our tendency to focus on negative events in our lives. We all fall victim to negative thinking, whether it is regrets about the past or worry anxieties about the future. Some people believe that the negativity bias is a protective safety measure that has a long evolutionary basis. My belief is that we

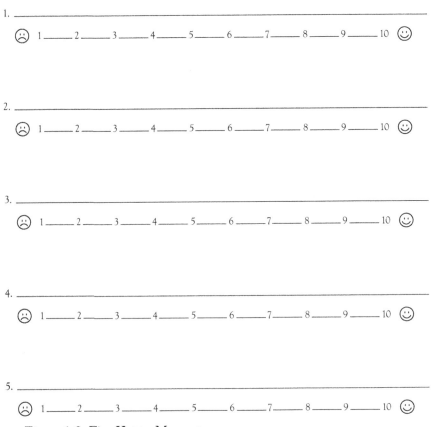

Figure 1.2 Five Happy Moments

all tend to focus on negatives far more than positives and that we have to train ourselves to focus more on the things we do well and succeed in than those things that drag us down.

Time for a New Paradigm

Change is difficult. We are invested in certain ways of thinking and behaving, and changing our actions can be both terrifying and frustrating.

In 1964, when over 42 percent of Americans smoked cigarettes, the US Surgeon General's report told the story of how smoking is directly related to rates of lung cancer. It took over 50 years for that rate of smoking to be reduced by half. Consider the idea that just 25 years ago, there were many workplaces where you might attend a meeting and nearly half the folks in that room would be smoking! Today, that won't happen and you won't even find smokers outside the building. Change can be difficult but it does happen.

We are creatures of habit and it is far easier to stick with our daily routines and customs than to break out of our daily patterns and try something new. When we do, however, we may very well find something more effective and enjoyable.

In conversations with employees at a utility company's call center, they reported that they rarely received calls thanking them for the electricity always being on. Instead the bulk of their calls were complaints about bills, missing repair reps, or emergencies. Emphasizing the idea that the call center staff's efforts should be to calm customer concerns by listening and seeking agreement first, actually worked to create a solution faster than trying to argue with customers or get them off the line. Suddenly, call center reps were charmers and the stress level for everyone was lower.

Changing perspectives is not easy but it *is* doable. We change perspectives on our worldview when one of three things happens:

1. *We face some life crisis or tragedy and see the world in a whole new way.* My friend George, who loved a diet of meat and potatoes, suffered a heart attack at age 56 and immediately became an evangelical vegetarian, spouting the virtues of a plant-based diet.
2. *We discover an undeniable truth.* A senior leader believed that he was the "golden boy" of the organization until he found out that the CEO thought he was rude and disrespectful in meetings and had his path for advancement closed.

3. *We seek a better outcome for ourselves.* Making a decision to act and behave differently can come out of recognition that we want our life to be different. Making that choice means that we begin to change the actions we take and the behaviors we manifest.

It's time to move on to try a new approach to dealing with our stress. Instead of trying to manage our stress and cursing our fate of a stress-filled life, let's see about a new way to experience and think about the stress in our lives. Let's start by recognizing and acknowledging that we are remarkably capable in the face of challenges and that we possess a vast array of skills in dealing with stress at home and at work. Our capabilities actually go well beyond just being able to manage our stress. We are built to not only survive through stress but to thrive through stress.

Case Study

A "hands-off" president of a division had a vice president who was a terror. He dressed people down in public, used inappropriate language, and constantly undermined his colleagues. He simply refused to be coached, saying, "I'm meeting my goals, my boss is happy, and this is who I am."

When I met with the president to share his subordinate's comments, he mentioned that the only downside of this problem was a high rate of turnover among lower level managers. I told him that was no real surprise and the bigger issue was how long the toxicity this VP was creating would infiltrate throughout the entire division.

"I understand what you are saying!" he told me. "But the truth is that this guy gets the job done and others who have tried were just too nice."

"Yes," I acknowledged. "But is this how you want to run your division? After all, everyone knows that you must condone this action and soon the way this plays out will not be good for you or him."

The subordinate was told that coaching was now being required. He refused to accept that decision and was let go within 30 days. Sometimes you have to focus on the person who *is* capable of change and is willing to step up to deal with the most challenging events.

CHAPTER 2

21st-Century Work Challenges: Bring Them On

In this chapter, we'll discuss the challenges of 21st-century living and working, and why, despite all our modern conveniences and resources, we seem to be more stressed than ever. We'll look at how we actually handle all that stress and discover an important element of the challenges in our lives . . . that we actually handle our stress pretty well and that our innate resilience capabilities keep us on balance and moving forward.

Furthermore, we'll show how the stress we face actually works for us in many situations and that it is not until we are through the challenge do we realize how important it was to us. Confronting the adversities we have in our lives and using our innate resilience capabilities create new learning pathways that help us take on future challenges in our lives. How would our lives be different if we didn't always seem to fight our stress but instead considered the opportunities being afforded to us?

We'll discuss how business, personal, and societal stresses are intimately linked and how our nation's ability to be resilient in the face of natural and man-made disasters connects with personal approaches to resilience.

The Stress Pandemic

"Reality is the leading cause of stress for those who are in touch with it."[v] Lily Tomlin's words are right on target and the reality of 21st-century challenges makes dealing with it more and more difficult. The truth is that reality can rough us up enough that we feel as if we've been battling a mixed-martial arts champion in the ring.

Living in a fast-paced world has its advantages and disadvantages for certain. It's great to Skype with your kids in the evening from their college dorm but not so great to talk to your Asian work colleague who asked you to attend a 1 p.m. China Standard Time meeting, which is 1 a.m. Eastern Daylight Time. Today's cars are amazing works of technology, but if that navigation system breaks down, you're probably looking at a $2,000 repair bill. Your company may be rolling out plans for a new capital investment, but that means a hiring freeze which translates into more work for everyone.

The rapid pace of change, along with technological advances that keep us connected globally and locally, leaves us little time for reflection and thinking. One of my colleagues told me that he's even had to stop listening to NPR radio on his way home, so that he can use that 30-minute block of time to think about what he achieved that day and what challenges await him tomorrow.

Several years ago, I facilitated a strategic planning retreat for a senior leadership team. We were able to spend a couple of days away from their workplace at a quiet resort where they could contemplate and consider the future. The planning session was great. When I ran into the CEO a year later, he asked me to come back and meet with the team, but we would be able to spend only a half-day working on their strategy and it would have to be at their office. When we discussed the session design, I pointed out that getting away from the office provided a time for thought and reflection, two necessary components of planning. Soon he saw that getting away from it all was more than a luxury. It was a necessary component for reflective thought. And thought has been in short supply these days because everyone is just trying to keep his or her head above water.

We've already experienced two great challenges in the 21st century, all within the first 15 years. The horror of 9/11 changed our perspective on global politics and the Great Recession of 2008 impacted our work and economic life.

While most of us understand the impact of 9/11 and recognize its influence on our world, for the most part, few of us are directly affected by the global war on terror. That is not the case for the Great Recession. Jobs were lost, careers were shattered, and the workplace has been changed forever.

A Leading Cause of Decreased Thinking: How Your Smart Phone Is Making You Stupid

Here's an experiment for you to try for the next 20 minutes.

- Make a note of the time right now.
- Continue reading this chapter.
- Make a note at the moment you feel an urge to check your smart phone.

I'd be willing to make a small wager that most of you will feel the urge to check your phone after about 10–15 minutes. I call it the "Connection Affection" because we want to stay in touch with everything that is going on in our lives. Our cell phone has become an anchor that helps us find stable ground but may also be weighing us down.

We've become habituated to our smart phones. While our devices provide amazing benefits they may also, unfortunately, be making us do stupid things. While we are doing great things like making bank deposits, watching a TED talk, or updating Evernote, we are also doing some really dumb things, like texting while driving 70 mph, checking e-mail during staff meetings, talking to a friend while having lunch with another friend, or waking up in the morning and verifying the outside temperature instead of opening the patio door.

Following the financial crisis in 2008, there was great uncertainty for everyone in the workplace. While unemployment is down, many high-paying jobs have not returned and employees who've received average merit increases of 1 percent over the past five years are telling their bosses that they are thrilled and appreciative of the bump even though the rate of inflation over that period has averaged 2 percent. They are still just happy to have a job. That wasn't the case for many of us.

It was a Monday morning back in March 2009 and I was headed down to my boss's office for our weekly check-in meeting. I knew we had a big layoff planned for the week and I had even reluctantly recommended two of my department's positions be downsized.

I was not prepared, however, when I walked into Frank's office and saw that our group's HR partner, Denise, was in there as well. It took me about three seconds to realize that I was also going to be downsized.

"Wow, I thought to myself. I can't believe this is really happening." I was having a kind of out-of-body experience. From the stress framework, I had moved into freeze response. I just sat there and took it all in.

Afterward I began thinking about what was happening. I'd had a very successful career. I'd been a highly capable psychologist, having helped thousands of people and families improve their life. I consulted with scores of companies on improving their organizational effectiveness, and I had built my own consulting and clinical business that I had successfully sold to a national health care company. On that day in March, I was finishing a 12-year career as a health care executive.

It took me a few months before I started realizing what a blessing all this was going to be. I recognized that I had achieved many of the goals I had set for myself in that role and that I was probably ready for a new challenge. That wasn't the case for the people who remained in their role during that period. I frequently heard from many of my former colleagues that all those layoffs made life miserable for anyone who was left.

Cutbacks meant more work for everyone. Mergers and acquisitions between and within corporations created expectations that employees have to be available 24/7. The pace of change accelerated which meant that projects that used to take nine months now had to be completed in three months. Managers are at a loss as to how to manage in this new world. Workplace engagement studies tell them that they have to be more supportive of their employees. They have to pay attention to generational issues between boomers and Millennials. Most Millennials not only want their workplace to be fun and respectful of their work–life balance, but they also expect to see their companies contributing to social problem solutions. Boomers want to have full engagement by everyone and are ready to stay to make sure the job gets done right. Managers are judged not only on how well their business group performs in terms of profit and loss figures, but also on how well they retain and grow their people.

From the employee side, it seems like only a small percent of people even enjoy their jobs. Research from The Gallup Organization showed that in 2014, approximately 29 percent of employees were engaged in their job. Fifty-one percent were not engaged, seeing their job as just a job, and close to 19 percent of employees see their workplace as a torture chamber.[vi] Glassdoor, a website that allows employees to rate employers, reported that only 54 percent of employees would recommend their company as a good place to work.[vii]

The 2015 American Psychological Association's annual survey on stress showed four main areas of stress: financial pressures and work-related stress where over 60 percent of respondents indicated a significant issue and family and health concerns where close to 50 percent of respondents reported challenges.[viii]

The stress research and all of our anecdotal experience tell us that we really are overwhelmed and that the tools we are using are just not working.

We Handle Our Stress Pretty Well

There is a dirty little secret that all the stress management teachers, wellness instructors, and even your physician don't want you to know. You actually handle your stressful life quite well.

We've become so programmed to think that we are incompetent at dealing with life's challenges that we rarely recognize or celebrate the achievements we make every day at overcoming life's big and small difficulties.

In the section above, we note that the American Psychological Association reports on an annual basis the level of stress in the U.S. population. Their report for 2015, entitled *Stress in America: Paying With Our Health*, sounds ominous, yet their report opens with the following sentence:

> Overall, Americans seem to be doing fairly well—average stress levels are trending downward (4.9 in 2014 vs. 6.2 in 2007 on a 10-point scale, where 1 is "little or no stress" and 10 is "a great deal of stress") and people generally say they are in good health (80 percent say their health is excellent, very good or good).[ix]

The report goes on to describe specific issues of stress-related problems for populations such as people in poverty, young adults, and parents—all coping with financial and emotional problems. It also points out that a gap exists between what people perceive to be a healthy level of stress (3.7 on a 10-point scale) and their current report stress level (which was 4.9).

One of our favorite parts of the report discusses the way stress symptoms affect people. The report highlights the fact that 75 percent of Americans report at least one stress symptom in the past month that might include feeling irritable, angry, anxious, decreased motivation, fatigue, or feeling sad.[x] Although we are not statisticians, we have to at least consider the possibility that if over three-quarters of the population is only experiencing one stress-related symptom a month, we are all doing relatively well in the face of our stressful lives.

In 1908, psychologists Robert Yerkes and John Dodson discovered through their research that increasing stress levels would increase performance.[xi] A bit of tension creates heightened performance. Think about stage actors who report feeling nervous but give a great performance. You probably find yourself anxious when presenting before your boss or colleagues but you usually pull it off well. Professional speakers are in this category.

Figure 2.1 shows the Yerke–Dodson curve as stress management experts typically represent it. The graph shows that there is just a small moment in time when the relationship between the amount of stress and performance meets. This drawing shows why stress management professionals suggest that there is a danger to our health and well-being whenever our stress level is actually too low or too high. Psychologists often will say that after the peak of the curve is reached, then it's all downhill.

In Figure 2.2, however, where we have relabeled the Yerkes–Dodson curve, it is possible to see that the graphical representation of how we deal with stress will be similar on the way down as it is on the way up. No one is "peak performing" all the time. On the way up, we sometimes need to just use more focus to increase our performance. On the way down, we sometimes need a bit more grit and stick-to-it-iveness to achieve our success. Yet psychologists and others always want to say that when we get over that hump, we are already in distress and health danger. We would say that it is only when we are at the tail ends of the curve that the risk of extreme boredom (on the left of the curve) or burn out and exhaustion (on the right side of the curve) enter the equation.

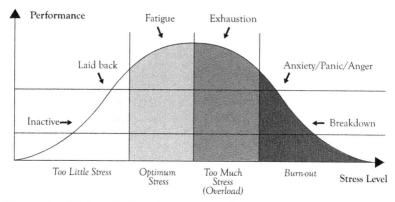

Figure 2.1 Yerkes–Dodson Stress Curve[xii]

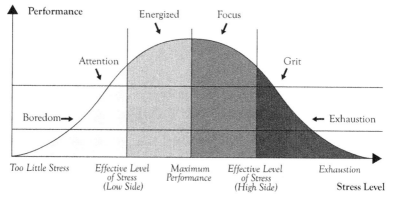

Figure 2.2 The Resilience Advantage Curve™

Case Study

We have a remarkable capacity to self-regulate the amount of stress we are capable of managing at any one time. In one of my client companies, they asked me to meet with manufacturing employees who were working night shifts during a three-month period. The managers were concerned about their stress levels because they had learned that many of these employees were also working second jobs.

When I met with the employees, they told me they worked second jobs to make some extra money since they had time off during the day.

continued

Given their financial situation, they truly felt they needed the extra income.

Asking them how they coped with two jobs, they told me that their spouses had agreed to help out with household chores and child management, so they could get some good sleep during their free time. They abandoned social activities for the most part and just dug down to focus on their two jobs.

When I reviewed workplace data with the managers, they told me that there was no increase in injuries or accidents, attendance was good, and the plant was meeting their production levels. While I think their concern about employee overload was warranted, the data we gathered all suggested that these employees were able to cope effectively with their self-imposed challenge.

The Great Differentiator: Looking for and Understanding Adversity

It was a little more than 100 years ago that Roald Amundsen, a Norwegian explorer, set out to be the first man to reach the North Pole. When he found out that Robert Peary and Frederick Cook had beaten him, he told a friend "probably something was left to be done." He clarified it a bit later by stating, "...there was nothing left for me but to try to solve *the last great problem*—The South Pole." He turned himself around and headed due south.[xiii]

Amundsen conquered the South Pole in 1911 with five colleagues and 52 dogs. He was no doubt a great explorer, but not a very good predictor. Today's explorers are uncovering many secrets, all of which are as challenging but perhaps not as dangerous as Amundsen's trek.

Modern day pioneers are no less driven to discover the unknown and to face the dangers inherent in doing so. Astronauts are compelled to go into space. Oceanographers want to understand the depths of the sea and research oncologists are racing to find cures for cancer. Each of these pioneers is accepting a challenge, knowing that there may be great odds working against his or her success. Yet they pursue these opportunities with great vigor.

I remember the first time I heard about Elon Musk's plan to build electric cars. Musk, a South African-born entrepreneur, made his fortune in the early days of the Internet. He decided to pursue his passion for alternative energy and space exploration. It was around 2008 when I first read about his ideas for creating a national network of electric car charging stations, much like today's gas stations. Soon his Tesla Roadster could be seen on California highways. Today, the high-end Model S is showing up all around the country and soon the Model X SUV, designed and priced for a large consumer market, will become a more common part of everyday traffic. Musk's Tesla Motors is trying to change the way we drive, at the same time making a contribution to keep Amundsen's South Pole intact.

Would you consider Musk to be just as much an explorer as Amundsen? Amundsen's exploration was life-threatening, whereas Musk's is certainly ego-threatening at the least, although his ego is what is probably required to build the first new car company in a couple of generations.

Even more impressive about these pioneers is that each signed up for these challenges. They weren't forced to pursue these dreams and ideals. Each recognized that without a challenge, without putting themselves into a high-stress position, neither they nor the world could advance.

In a way, each of us is an explorer in our own lives. As a youngster, you have to decide on what college to attend or what kind of job you will pursue. As adults, we have the opportunity to decide whether we will pursue a path that might be harder but also more rewarding. Choosing to battle adversity is never an easy path, but it may oftentimes be a rewarding one.

Choosing to take on a challenge is different from having adversity choose you. Much of our stress comes from factors that seem out of our control. Daily travails like traffic, time crunches, bad bosses, and the like are all difficulties we have to face and overcome every day. Greater life challenges also come our way, such as a loss of our job, a family divorce, or an untimely death. This is what, in part, distinguishes acute or current stress from ongoing or chronic stress. Both are dangerous and both can be taken on and beaten.

In our resilience approach, we'll seek to see these challenges as a normal part of life and will discuss ways that we can normalize them, so that they take on solely the level of importance that they deserve. For sure, losing a job or going through a divorce is of major import and the difficulties of those events take a significant toll on us physically, mentally, and emotionally. Yet, if you look back on the kinds of difficulties you've faced, you will probably come to the conclusion, as I have, that we handle these situations rather effectively. Perhaps not always gracefully but we almost always get through them in a way in which we can look back and feel proud of what and how we did.

Furthermore, we usually gain a perspective not too long after the event occurred that it was "perhaps one of the best things that ever happened to me." I know that was the case for me when I lost my job back in 2009 and when other difficulties have come my way. I've learned to step back and ask the question, "what is the learning in all this for me and can I take advantage of it?" Even in the face of significant life challenges, that question may be the only one worth asking and answering.

Going beyond how we face certain adversities about which we may not have any choice is the question of whether we should put ourselves into situations where we stress our bodies even more. What, if like Amundsen, Musk, and other great leaders, we are also provided the opportunity to *intentionally* go after challenges? We test our mettle to see how we do in the face of difficulties. A friend of mine recently completed his first marathon. "Twenty-six miles, 385 yards," he kept telling me. He shared his training regimen that went back six months before the race. He went on early morning runs in winter's darkness. He would hope for snow, so that he could work on his agility in keeping his balance on slippery sidewalks. Spring rains were invigorating, as he knew that race day could leave him wet and soggy. He even traveled south for a half-marathon preparatory run, so that he could get used to hot and humid conditions, just in case that was the condition on his day.

He did great on race day, tired and weary, but something inside him told him that he took on the challenge, endured the stress, and overcame the difficulty.

He was experiencing his joy of overcoming his self-imposed stress.

Resilience as Part of Our Fabric

In 1955, there were 698 children born on the Island of Kauai in Hawaii. As part of a research team that included pediatricians, and public health care workers, psychologist Emmy Werner wanted to watch how these children developed over the course of their lifetime and what factors contributed to their successes and failures as adults. This kind of longitudinal study is rare, but when done properly it provides enormous insight into what factors are critical to life success.

One of the study's key hypotheses was that children who experienced both biological prenatal risk factors (such as premature birth or mothers who abused drugs during pregnancy) along with postnatal challenges (mentally ill parents or absent fathers) would experience more difficulties as teenagers and adults than children born to more stable homes. About a third of the children born to this cohort group met the criteria for being born into an impoverished environment.

Over the course of the next 40 years, what happened was documented and published in a number of books such as *The Children of Kauai* [xiv] and *Vulnerable but Invincible*.[xv] Werner and her other researchers found that about two-thirds of the children born to that sub-cohort group experienced significant life challenges such as learning disabilities, substance abuse, and chronic unemployment as adults. The remaining one-third grew up to become competent, fully functioning adults with meaningful jobs, and happy families. For this group, by age 40, none had been incarcerated, drug dependent, or showed any of the negative events reported by the other sub-cohort group. In an article published by Portland State University, Professor Werner noted about the successful children:

> Their very existence challenges the myth that a child who is a member of a so-called "high risk" group is fated to become one of life's losers.[xvi]

Emmy Werner and her team identified what they called "protective factors" that created resilience in each of these surviving children leading them to become thriving adults. These factors focused on individual capabilities such as being more sociable as infants, becoming readers as children, and confidence in themselves as teens. These children received familial support through developing a close relationship with an emotionally stable adult such as an aunt or uncle who provided security and support. Their community supports included an understanding teacher or minister to whom they could turn to for help. In fact, most of these children had a significant crisis as teenagers and they were able to use their resources to help them overcome their adversity. These events often created a turning point for them where they recognized that they were able to overcome their challenges and could succeed in the face of adversity.

While Werner and her colleagues identified a cultural basis for resilience, two physician researchers, Steven Southwick and Dennis Charney wrote about the biological basis for resilience in their book, *Resilience: The Science of Mastering Life's Greatest Challenges*, which Southwick summarized in a popular article in 2012 called "The Science of Resilience."[xvii]

Their research based on studying posttraumatic stress disorder and more catastrophic personal and societal events identified numerous ways the body responds to stress and adversity in a resilient manner including:

- When experiencing a stressful event, our nervous system is activated and releases stress hormones, including epinephrine, norepinephrine, and cortisol. These hormones create the heightened awareness, rapid heartbeat, and change in our breathing that quickly helps us address the stressor. However, these hormones turn off just as quickly as they turn on, allowing our body to return to a normal state so that we return to a balanced state of being.
- Even when we are experiencing chronic rounds of stress, we can still find pleasure and joy in specific situations. After a funeral, a family gathers to share stories, food, and friendship. Laughter fills the room as everyone recalls the beauty of the person who was lost. It seems as if our nervous system won't routinely let us stay in a negative place forever and will release coping hormones like dopamine or oxytocin, so that we can experience some joy and companionship.
- As we'll see as we explore strategies for resilience, we are capable of thinking our way into planning strategies around

stress and developing ways to recover from challenging events. Research using EEGs and functional MRIs show that certain resilience strategies, such as cognitive reframing, mindfulness meditation, and even short-term planning, activate our left prefrontal cortex and help mitigate stressful situations.

- Most people report that physical exercise helps them diminish their stress level. Some people say that by working out after a stressful day, it helps rid their body of the negative energy that's accumulated over the day. Others, who might like to get up early and work out first thing in the morning, report their fitness activities seem to build up extra energy they draw on during the course of that challenging day. Southwick reports that studies with both animals and people show that vigorous physical exercise helps grow nerve cells in specific parts of the brain and that it lowers the level of stress hormones in the hippocampus, a part of the brain that plays a role in regulating hormonal response to the stress reaction.[xviii]

How do you rate yourself on your inherent resilience qualities? Consider some of these questions below and write down your own experiences about your personal and family history in dealing with stress.

1. How do you typically handle stressful situations? Do you feel you are able to cope effectively? Or do you run away or even get mad and frustrated when you have to deal with tense situations? What is your natural tendency toward stress?

_____

_____

_____

2. How did you see your parents and relatives handle challenging situations? What are the family stories about how your relatives overcame (or did not overcome) adverse situations?

_____

_____

_____

3. When you think about stressful situations that might come up for you in the future, do you feel like you have an effective approach? Or do you feel like every situation is one where you just have to "wing it?"

---

4. Do you feel like you do healthy activities that allow you to deal with your stress situations in a more effective manner? Write down what it is that you do. How/why you think it improves your ability to deal with your stress?

---

5. Do you consider yourself to be a resilient person? Why? Provide examples of how you've demonstrated resilience. Why do you think you are or are not resilient?

The research and our experience tell us that resilience is hardwired into our systems. Unlike the stress management model that wants us to believe that we do not know how to deal with our stressors, *the evidence is that most of us deal effectively with life challenges successfully*. As we explore more about how resilience can help you achieve a greater measure of awareness and control over how you deal with stress, we'll continually return to the strengths you already bring to the resilience table.

Our National Perspective: Connecting Community, Business, and Personal Resilience

We all watched with anticipation and concern as Mayor Ray Nagin finally took the action that was required. By then, however, it was too late. The Mayor of New Orleans had been given warnings from the National Weather Service and from local weather experts in New Orleans for several days, but his decision to keep the evacuation voluntary meant that many of the over 100,000 residents who did not have transportation could not find ways out of the City. Nagin's approach to the hurricane's preparation was to tell folks that he "didn't want to panic anyone" but that they should consider leaving the city. It was not until his 10 a.m. news conference on Sunday, August 28, 2006 that he finally ordered an emergency evacuation of the Big Easy. Less than 24 hours later, Katrina struck New Orleans and the damage to the people of that city was felt clear across the country.[xix]

Contrast that to the approach taken by Governor Chris Christie on October 27, 2012, when the Governor of New Jersey ordered the evacuation of New Jersey's barrier islands and Atlantic City a full two days before Hurricane Sandy reached the Jersey shore. In contrast to Nagin, Christie's imperative left no doubt about his expectations for the hurricane or what his response to people who choose to stay behind. The Governor's message was clear. Residents who opted to stay should plan on being on their own for up to a week with no power, outside sources of food or water,' or help from first responders.

"You will be on your own," he told them and acknowledged that the government and even local first responders would not be able to risk resources to save people in danger during those first few days. In fact, he informed them that he was not prepared to put first responders' lives in danger for those people who ignore the evacuation warning. Christie's language was clear: "Get the hell out of there."[xx]

While comparisons between hurricanes and preparations for them may not be completely fair (since damage from Katrina was primarily the result of the failure of the levees to hold rather than the direct impact of the storm), the results of not ordering people out of a community before danger hits are unmistakable. The failure to act ahead of the crisis led to a loss of life across Katrina's swatch 16 times greater than the loss of life from Hurricane Sandy, despite a much higher population in the Northeast.

Even more striking about the two disasters is how communities learned from natural disasters such as Katrina and applied that knowledge to Hurricane Sandy. In the space of the past 15 years, governments and communities have come to terms with their limitations. No longer do they assume that their resources can really make a difference in the face of destructive natural and man-made events. Instead, the approach is to prepare by anticipating that these kinds of events will happen, get people out of the way, stockpile goods, supplies, and emergency support away from the point of impact, and be ready to jump in to help out as soon as the crisis has past.

This shift in thinking actually occurred after 9/11. Government reports, including the 9/11 Commission's summary finding, specifically stated that the United States should strive to be *more resilient.*[xxi] This goal came out of the recognition that no matter how strong our nation is and how many resources we may pour into a specific objective, we cannot keep bad things from happening. This seemingly obvious statement may very well have been overlooked by many in government, business and in communities. As a result, a number of national and community-based organizations have taken the initiative to educate and implement strategies for building community resilience across the country.

One such organization working to address these low-potential but high-destruction events has been the Rockefeller Foundation. They initiated a $100 million effort to build resilience across 100 global cities, helping them develop local community resilience strategies. In addition to workshops and training sessions, each city is funded to hire a "Chief Resilience Officer" who develops a plan, accesses tools for community resilience, and identifies resources that will help regional urban centers be more prepared to respond to natural and man-made disasters. At a recent planning conference, it was noted that for every $1 spent on preparation and mitigation associated with natural disasters, the saving is $4 on post-disaster recovery.[xxii]

At the kickoff of the Resilience Project in New Orleans in 2013, the current mayor of New Orleans, Mitch Landrieu, spoke about the importance of community resilience. "We almost lost an entire American city and people gasped at the extent of the damage," he said. "[The hurricane] eviscerated the city and people asked, 'what's wrong with the people of New Orleans?' People thought we did something wrong. But we're really the canary in the coal mine."[xxiii]

Of course, it's not just governments and communities that recognize the limitations we have over natural and man-made events. Businesses are also focused on how to be resilient in facing their challenges. Recent cyber-attacks on Target, Anthem, and Sony Pictures demonstrate not only how companies must tighten up their own security features to create less vulnerability but also how they must "bounce back" from the public's perception of how well the company is managing their internal operations.

It's not just big and unpredictable events that demand organizational resilience but also regularly predictable events that happen to companies where they must find a way to address them in the public sector. On May 1, 2015, the CEO of Burlington Northern Santa Fe Railway, Matt Rose, came on television to question the cost of new government regulations requiring his and other railway companies to build and retrofit rail cars. This was to ensure that petroleum shipped from the U.S. West to refining plants in Texas and Louisiana would be safe from explosions due to derailments. Rose recognized the importance of this improvement, but pointed out that BNSF and the other railways ship millions of barrels of oil every year without any incident, and the costs of these new improvements would impact the capacity of the company to ensure that there were enough rail cars to deliver needed oil to U.S. refiners and customers.[xxiv]

Five days later, a BNSF train carrying petroleum derailed, causing a massive fire near the rural town of Heimdel, North Dakota. This event, like others across the continent, has spurred concerns about how well the rail industry is able to manage the transport of oil and is the reason that the government has been forced to intervene.

BNSF was on the scene quickly in Heimdel and local citizens there complimented the company for its quick and rapid response to the disaster. BNSF established a disaster recovery center within hours of the crash and had a plan in place to clean up the site and ensure that citizens were safe from any toxic fumes or leaks.[xxv]

Like thousands of companies that now have disaster recovery programs in place, BNSF was focused on putting their emergency response plan in action to ensure that they and their rail lines are resilient in the face of this accident.

Corporate resilience typically focuses on an array of areas that create vulnerability in corporations. These typically include the following:

- Business continuity—what happens if fire or floods destroy a manufacturing or other key resource?
- IT cyber-attacks

- Security breach, such as corporate theft or even workplace violence
- A workplace failure that does not result in improvement even when an improvement plan is in place
- Operational failures, such as poor-performing software, or a lack of resources, such as unfilled positions or dated hardware
- A negative event that creates bad publicity and potential loss of business
- Sudden loss of a key executive or group

Companies recognize the impact of these types of crises to their workplace. While CFOs might cite financial losses as the most critical factors, a 2014 Forrester Research report on business resilience pointed out that the business leaders surveyed reported that the greatest impact of these kinds of disruptions impacts people, not profits. Seventy-two percent of companies reported a loss of employee productivity and 37 percent reported a loss of employee morale.[xxvi]

These findings are interesting in that most of the dollars spent to address resilience in the workplace *do not go to people resilience but instead to infrastructure and process management improvements*. It certainly makes sense to build resilience into operational structures, but few companies have embraced how to support creating resilient people.

We'll start to do that next.

CHAPTER 3

The Resilience Revolution: The Teflon for Stress

Our learning about life does not come from the degrees we acquire but from the experiences we accrue. If we are lucky, these experiences challenge and push us to accomplish things we never thought we could do, and which often create a great deal of stress in so doing.

That's not the idea that's been sold to us. We learn that we should avoid stressful situations in all cases and hope that we have a life that is easy and relaxing because it is best for our well-being and health. I'm pretty sure that even the crown princes and princesses in Europe had plenty of stressful situations. Heck, some of them even had to worry about losing their heads, literally.

Instead, we should find a way to recognize and embrace the stressful situations, recognizing that there will be times in our lives when stress will be high, and then be ready to navigate those turbulent waters in a conscious and mindful manner. The Hellsgate Bridge in New York City allowing trains to cross the East River is from the Dutch for "turbulent waters." We need such bridges ourselves. Accomplishing that objective will then help us see ways to learn from our experiences, so that we are not just bouncing back but also streaming forward.

This can help create an expanded definition of resilience as being our ability to effectively plan for such progress, navigate successfully, and gracefully recover from those challenging events in such a way that we are strengthened by the experience. We want to travel above the roiling waters below.

Getting the Juices Going

What constitutes your greatest learning? Counter-intuitively, perhaps, the source won't be school. The source would be experiences, victories, defeats, people, experimentation, and serendipity. Our major learning is "life learning," *provided we're capable and willing to look around, appreciate what's happening, and be wise enough to ask questions about what it all means to us.*

Most great successes are opportunistic. The individual recognizes an opportunity and reacts swiftly to it. We're forced to pay attention in school (especially in days past) because the teachers demanded strict discipline. You *had* to pay attention or suffer the consequences of a call home to mom and dad. You might be distracted, but you found a way to hide it. There are no such strictures for life today, and many people simply don't pay attention or are distracted by the abundant stimuli around them.

But learning of any sort creates stress. Typical developments in formalized learning such as these created stress for most of us when we were students:

- Standardized tests
- A change in curriculum or teacher
- Joining a club and having to meet new people
- A pop quiz
- Having to present a report in front of the whole class

The same phenomenon holds true in our jobs and careers:

- Hearing that you'll be getting a new boss
- Having meetings with perspective new clients
- Finding out that your company is increasing insurance premiums
- Getting a promotion
- Project deadlines

Any one of these challenges is going to create stress, but after you've tackled any one or all of them, you've developed strategies on how to deal with them. Even if you are far from perfect in your effort, each successive effort will bring you closer to success. These challenges actually serve to get biological "juices" or hormones flowing, and to help create the creative ideas, energy, and persistence that help us achieve our goals.

These reactions are biochemical and biological in nature, part of our natural voluntary and involuntary response systems. Yet we've become inured to the fact that they are harmful and negative. Of course, they can be dangerous if they are persistent and are maintained at high levels, and this can be the case in many situations. Learning to take control of your stress by building resilience will help identify when these levels are beginning to reach perilous levels.

The best performers use stress to improve themselves. Star athletes are those who perform best under stress those who seek the ball when the clock is running out. Hall of Fame former center for the Boston Celtics, Bill Russell, wrote a book called *Second Wind* in which he describes that the true mark of a champion is performing at one's absolute best under the greatest possible pressure.[xxvii] Joe Montana, the legendary quarterback for the San Francisco 49ers, always wanted to be calling the plays in the last two minutes of a close game. He usually won.

Thus, it becomes a matter of perspective. Do we see pressure as an opportunity to excel or as a threat to our existence? If we've been "taught" stress is threatening, we can "teach" ourselves how to accept it more positively and use it. Thus, the salesperson who is prepared for the skeptical customer's questions, or the executive needing to make a deal on an acquisition before next week's board meeting, or a front-desk clerk who sees an upset guest and works to soothe his or her concerns before he or she escalates. The truth is that no one is shooting at us and much of the stress we experience may very well be created in our own mind.

One challenge that we'll work on in this book is to change our perception of stress from always being negative to often being positive. We'll have to work to override the biologically imperative stress reaction, but if we can begin to make that shift in our favor, we'll begin to create more ease, creativity, and effectiveness. We'll be spending less time worrying and more time enjoying. All this begins by assuming we are in danger when experiencing stress, instead of seeing it as an opportunity.

This may seem like a strange notion, but it is one that we have actually heard about and lived in our own lives. Veteran actors and singers churn with stress just before generating a great performance. Lady Gaga, Adele, and even Justin Bieber, have numerous episodes of getting physically ill before their live performances, but then go on to perform magnificently. Newspaper reporters procrastinate until an hour before a deadline, and then write award-winning pieces. In the workplace, we might pace up and down the hall waiting for our time to present a novel idea to our bosses, sure that we are going to bomb, but finding out that we hit it out of the park.

In all those situations our stress helped us perform well, even though we might have worried incessantly about how all of it would work out. The mental exercise of regarding stress as a friend, not an enemy, and as a launching pad, not quicksand, is all that you need to create gold out of formerly perceived adversity.

Does Stress Distress You?

The Franklin Roosevelt line about "fearing fear itself" is brilliant, because it's like the dark room that people fear just because, well, it's a dark room. At an amusement park when Alan's kids were young, his son refused to go into a dark room.

"Don't be afraid of the dark," Alan told him.

"I'm not afraid of the dark," he assured.

"Then why won't you go in?" Alan asked.

"Because of what might be in the dark."

I find that to be a highly rational response.

Stress is no different. We fear it because it's there. Stress is actually "neutral." We've explained how stress can be turned into opportunity and gain, and the value of eustress or positive stressors. Stress is a reaction to stimuli (an event of some sort), but that stimuli needn't automatically cause a negative reaction. Our reaction—and however we control or don't control it—causes the stress.

A person pulling out a gun, or smoke coming from the next room, can cause highly negative stress. But even in those conditions, if you allow the stress to overcome your rationality—to panic—you'll almost certainly succumb to the worst possibilities. Similarly, you might win a lottery or be chosen for a promotion–sudden stimuli that should cause stress of a different kind. Although you might think this is a no-brainer to deal with, many who win fortunes squander them quickly, and many promotions— have wound up in drunken binges and lost friends.

Correlation is not cause. That is, we often mistakenly attribute a direct relationship between stress and reaction, but there are actually many me-diators in between, no different from trying to contact the president of a company. There are myriad others to go through who may affect the route positively or negatively.

Richard Lazarus and Susan Folkman describe what they call the "Transactional Model," which describes stress as being *the imbalance between demands (stressor) and our resources (coping with the stressor).*[xxviii]

In that model:

A) Individuals coping with stress must first decide if the stressor is threatening or positive and whether it's actually relevant to one's situation. They call this the *primary appraisal.*

B) Once an individual determines the danger level, then they can decide if they have the resources to deal with it themselves or if they need extra help from outsiders (*secondary appraisal*).

C) If they can solve it themselves, then we go about using a problem-solving approach to resolving the issue.

D) When the stressor seems greater than the person's capacity to handle it, then an emotional response kicks in and the individual starts to feel overwhelmed and unable to cope with the problem effectively.

E) Often the choices made may lead to avoidance, anger, submission, or negative strategies like alcohol or drugs.[xxix]

In this last area, we're particularly concerned because we feel least in control, and lack of control has high negative stress implications. Hence, the very negative resolution attempts (drugs, anger, and even suicide).

However, people often misperceive and underestimate their ability to deal with such "perceived lack of control" and, consequently, it's their thinking that needs to change. The remedy in business is to help that change occur, so that people have more options and precedent for success.

In business, we call this "empowerment," which has become a hackneyed phrase; but we define empowerment in this manner: the ability to make decisions, which influence the outcomes of one's work.

You've no doubt experienced front-line personnel who can help you instantly—on the phone, in e-mail, in a store—who don't have to check with a supervisor. The best hotel operations—Four Seasons, Peninsula, the Mandarin Oriental—are famous for enabling room service deliverers, bellmen, valets, and desk clerks to make immediate decisions for unhappy customers or unusual requests. On a recent trip to the Four Seasons in Palm Beach, the front-desk clerk called to see if I needed help with my bags the night before checkout and then offered to get me my boarding passes for my flight home.

People are far more productive when stress is seen positively; therefore, empowerment in all businesses should be a fundamental principle of management. We can see these patterns in many organizations. Just talk to employees and listen for whether they have to refer challenges "up the ladder" and await an answer that may cause them negative stress with the customer, or whether they are positively engaged in finding a solution themselves.

We can't allow ourselves or our businesses to fall into the trap of fearing stress per se. We need to focus on the possibilities, challenges, and opportunities that new stimuli can bring. After all, a problem solved is the greatest testimonial to quality.

No one goes home bragging about a hotel that served their breakfast accurately and on time. They cite the hotel whose people are fast to correct inadvertent errors with speed and accuracy.

Going After the Gusto of Stress

We're often "searching for stress in all the wrong places." What if we started to look for stress in all the right places?"

Why do you work?

- To make money
- To be useful with your time
- To satisfy affiliation needs
- To make a contribution to improve society
- To receive benefits like health care
- To receive acclaim and accolades
- To learn from others
- To help people
- To be challenged to do your best

For most of us, there are always parts of our job that are fun and parts that are not fun. How do we increase the former and decrease the latter?

As a coach of long-standing, one of the first questions I ask a new client is, "Are you having fun?" That causes them to think, and it tells me a great deal in the first 30 seconds.

If we can find more of what we enjoy, even though it may be stressful, it will be enjoyable. Research shows that about one-third of employees love what they do, are highly engaged in their work, and see themselves as making important contributions.[xxx] These people make better use of their time, are more productive, and enjoy their work more.

We think about 50 percent of employees are moderately engaged, see their work as something they have to do to support their family, and look for ways to find satisfaction in their job. They hold themselves back from fully engaging because they do not want to "work too hard" but in doing so, miss out on finding meaning in what they do.

That leaves about 20 percent of employees who are disengaged, hate what they do, and can't wait to leave for the day or forever. These employees actively *work to not work*. They find ways to be absent from work, leave as early as possible, and maybe even undermine the effectiveness of the workplace. These people are energy suckers and are stress makers for others. They may not have more stress than others, but they create more of it for themselves and most of it for others.

I was meeting with a senior manager in the U.S. Justice Department, who described how passionate she was working with her clients, who were former inmates within the federal justice system. She was always looking for ways to help these men and women return to society and to help them find meaningful employment and the opportunity to create a happy home life.

Case Study

While consulting with an American auto manufacturer some years ago, Alan asked about large, various-sized wrenches in a case. "Oh, that's a forty-minute wrench," the guy on the assembly line said.

"Since when are wrenches measured in time units?" Alan asked, thinking the worker was pulling his leg.

"Since we know that's how long that wrench will stop the line if we drop it into that slot in the floor."

Her employees, as career government workers, did not always share her passion. We discussed her team members and what she discovered was that the engagement research cited above applied to her team locally. She recognized the challenge she had in changing the mindset of government workers (who could not be fired for their low performance) by creating more challenge in their job.

She helped her employees understand more about who they were as professionals and helped them to better understand their mission. She focused on building a team where each person did what they did best and encouraged them to do what they did best and enjoyed most.

While the level of stress and pressure was not significant, it was subtle and her persistence in ensuring that her team continued to focus on how they could help their clients eventually led to improved performance and participation. *Ironically, it was easier to engage the former inmates than it was her civilian employees.*

Take a look at your organization and recognize that you probably have the same percentage of engagement within your work group. The level of stress created in the workplace is, in large measure, based on the level of commitment and focus that your less engaged employees contribute.

We all have choices we can make. When Alan was fired, without much severance, by a tyrannical owner, he could have become distraught, angry, or frozen. His choice was to become angry vowing that no one would ever have that power over him again. When he made his decision, he realized that he had to be serious and disciplined about his decision. He proceeded to build a franchise around his ideas.

Along with choices, we are often too afraid of risk. We should *weigh* risk and reward, not flee from it. Nassim Nicholas Taleb, in his book, *The Black Swan*, calls this the "upside and downside."[xxxi] If we start to evaluate the risks that confront us in different stressful situations, one clear piece of fact finding usually comes through. There is remarkably less downside risk to the actions we might take in any particular situation (Figure 3.1).

Here's a risk/reward model for business and one for personal experiences. Consider the kinds of challenges you face at work and at home and rate the potential of the best thing happening and the worst thing

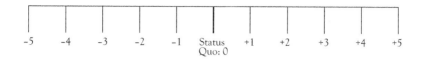

Question 1: *What is the best and worst that might result?*

Question 2: *What is the probability for success for this project?*

+5= Paradigm-breaking improvement, industry leader.
+4= Dramatic improvement, major publicity.
+3= Strong benefits, organization-wide.
+2= Minor benefits, localized.
+1= Very minor improvement, barely noticed.

−1= Very minor setback, barely noticed.
−2= Minor setback, controlled locally.
−3= Public setback, requires damage control.
−4= Major defeat, financial damages, recovery time needed.
−5= Devastating losses.

Figure 3.1 Risk/Reward: **Business**

+5= Transformational shift in my life like winning the lottery
+4= Dramatic improvement that creates notable success at work and home
+3= Successful gain that brings me praise and appreciation from others
+2= Success that is short lived but enjoyable
+1= Creates a good feeling but not much beyond it

−1= Minor setback, does not affect me much
−2= Problematic event, but easily managed within my immediate world
−3= A public setback, one that impacts my reputation
−4= A major defeat in an area that I have devoted much energy
−5= Major blow to finances, reputation or health.

Figure 3.2 Risk/Reward: Personal

happening. This allows you to put risk in perspective and to ask *a number of vital questions to gain control and utilize stress correctly:*

1. What can I do to prevent the likelihood of a negative event occurring?
2. What can I do to mitigate the effects if it does occur?
3. What can I do to create a positive outcome?
4. How do I build momentum to make that happen?

This model enables us to focus on the positives and potential wins by acknowledging and managing the negatives and potential losses. No one is shooting at us. Failure is seldom fatal.

Consider the challenges you've already taken on in your work and life. It might have been a new project, a promotion, a family relocation, running for office, coaching a team, and so forth. Regardless of the outcomes (no coach wins every game, no promotion is absolutely smooth), we learn from the entire experience. The experiences add more stress to our lives, but also more gusto and enjoyment. The conventional wisdom is "not to take on too many changes at once." But that's not true if you can use the inevitable stress to learn, improve, and have fun.

I've told people they shouldn't be agitated before addressing an audience. They should be anticipatory and eager. That's the positive use of the inexorable stress that develops. You may not feel that you understand everything happening in your work, particularly when your work or position changes. But if you simply act as if change is a constant (it is) and even volatility is familiar (it should be by this point), then you will increase the odds that all will work out.

Eventually, if we are psychologically healthy (and this book is intended to make you healthier about the use of stress), everything works out. You may not understand the nuances of underwriting, or soccer strategy, or remote sales, but you will. In the meantime, you can participate, watch, enjoy, and grow.

Expanding the Definition

Stress is sticky. We have a hard time letting go of it. Why is this? Because it creates these "normal" reactions:

- It makes us angry.
- It frustrates us.
- It hangs around like a bad guest.
- It wears us down.

Resilience changes our perspective on stress in that it moves us from a state of pain to a state of gain. The "normal" reaction is not one of desolation and helplessness.

We're creating a new definition of resilience that allows our stress to go through our bodies and out of us rather than taking up residency inside us and causing us pain. We're building a Teflon-based approach to stress, the same ones that successful politicians (Bill Clinton), athletes (Serena Williams), executives (Jamie Dimon), entrepreneurs (Jeff Bezos), entertainers (Taylor Swift), and every day successful people use, consciously or unconsciously. We want to bring it to a level of "conscious competency."

The term "resilience" crosses many different disciplines and means different things across those fields.

In engineering, the term resilience means the capacity of an object to absorb energy, resist the impact of that energy, and return to its previous state quickly. Consider the state of bridges across the country that are now under scrutiny because their core engineering structure has weakened due to years of poor or no maintenance. These bridges, while once resilient, have slowly lost their structural integrity.

In business, resilience is the ability of an organization to withstand the impact of some kind of strategic or operational disruption and continue its work while remedying the problem. Some companies were successful in the face of disruptions, while others were not:

- Blockbuster Video failed to see the leap from store-driven DVD video to streaming videos and declared bankruptcy in 2010. Netflix, on the other hand, effectively moved from mail-based DVDs to streaming-based movies successfully and is now driving streaming video in an entirely new way.
- Netflix's transformation has barely started. Their self-developed content is so popular and available on any personal device that many cable customers are "cutting the cord" and watching movies and video series just on their personal devices.

Of course, our area of focus is on health, psychology, and business and in these areas, resilience is typically defined as *an individual's ability to bounce back from stress and adversity.* Resilience for people is not about avoiding the stressors *but finding the capacity to deal with the stress in the best way possible.*

While resilience crosses many fields of study and has become a hot topic of late, perhaps it's time to reevaluate its meaning. We are proposing a new, pragmatic definition of resilience that is transformational. We believe that resilience is:

> *Our ability to effectively plan for, navigate successfully, and gracefully recover from challenging and stressful events in such a way that we are strengthened by the experience.*

This definition begins to change our perspective on resilience from merely looking at how we *cope* with stress to examining how we *use* these experiences to *grow* beyond what we realized we were capable of achieving.

The actress Diane Lane must have had a great approach to stress and certainly understood resilience. She was once quoted as saying, "I think the secret to happiness is having a Teflon soul. Whatever comes your way, you either let it slide or cook with it."[xxxii]

We're going to start cranking up the stove.

PART 2

The Rhythms of Resilience

Stress is all around us. It may strike in the middle of the night or on our drive to work. Sometimes it creates a feeling of panic and anxiety; other times a sense of desperation and worry. It seems like we can't escape and even if our stress strategy is effective in dealing with it one time, soon the stress feeling will strike again and knock us off balance.

Whether or not our stress reaction has a pattern, we want to develop a way to deal with stress as healthfully as possible. We need a cadence or rhythm to resilience that keeps us aware of potential challenges and how stress may affect us. Organizations can also help create this cadence.

We can think about our strategy for dealing with stress as occurring across a temporal continuum. The *Resilience Continuum*™ puts our stressful situations into a time framework that helps us address stress before it happens, while it is happening, and after it is over.

- The Resilience Continuum is composed of three elements:
  - How we prepare for stressful situations and build hardiness in the face of stressful situations.
  - How we navigate stressful situations in real time.
  - How we recover and learn from our stressful situations, so that we learn and grow from them.

Preparation

The 2012 Japanese earthquake and resulting tsunami brought ruin to communities in Northeastern Japan. The worst-case fears were tempered by the knowledge that Japan is the most prepared nation on the planet for natural

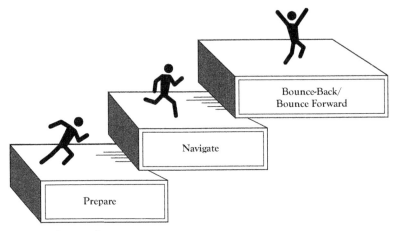

The Resilience Continuum

disasters and that the Japanese people knew what to do when the warning sirens went off. As far back as the mid-1950s, Japan began a campaign of educating their population about the effects of earthquakes and tsunamis. Buildings are reinforced, sea walls are strengthened, and well-marked evacuation routes signs are displayed. But far and away, the most important element of the preparation is the constant training the Japanese children and adults receive in preparation for such cataclysmic events. As a result, while the loss of life from this event ran well into thousands, it wasn't tens of thousands, as has happened in other parts of the world.

Although we might do some preparation for potential disasters, these high-risk but low-occurrence events usually fly under our radar as far as preparatory actions. More frequent stress events that usually have lower impact are the ones that affect most of our days, but rarely do we think about how we can mitigate or even eliminate the predictable stress that usually accompanies these daily activities. A recent research report told the story of why business, scientific, and political leaders like Mark Zuckerberg, Albert Einstein, and President Obama tended to wear the same style clothing every day. Eliminating the need to make clothes selections beyond a standard dress code (Zuckerberg's gray t-shirt, Einstein's and Obama's blue suits) allowed them to simplify their morning ritual and focus their energy on more important matters. Preparing for a challenging day by taking away energy-draining activities allows a clearer focus on what is important. Rituals and routines are important tools in getting in front of our predictable stressors. We'll consider all the ways preparation can help you in the next chapter.

If we can prepare for tsunamis, we can prepare for our own challenging days.

Navigation

In a recent blog post, Paul Sullivan, the author of *Clutch*, discussed what it takes to deliver great results in the midst of a pressure-filled situation. He describes the challenge facing the University of Connecticut women's basketball team as they played for a record setting 89th consecutive victory—a victory that would establish a new NCAA record for most consecutive wins. Sullivan's observation of successful athletes points to one key factor in how people navigate through stress-filled events.[xxxiii]

His research showed that the ability to focus and be *present in the moment* is critical to successfully navigating our most challenging situations. Most of us will not be able to maintain the cool showed by Maya Moore, Connecticut's star basketball forward, but we can improve our ability to become resilient in many stressful situations.

By developing the skill of "maintaining attention" to what we are doing, we are able to be present in the moment, a key element of "being clutch" and also being able to navigate through a challenging situation. This is the heart of what we all strive to do when we talk about "managing stress." It's not about eliminating the anxiety or worry, but about recognizing the pressure we are feeling is real. Developing the skill to use that pressure to help us stay present in each moment helps us perform better.

Bounce Back or Perhaps Bounce Forward

Pittsburgh is a city that knows a lot about resilience. In the early 1900s, Pittsburgh was the Silicon Valley of our country. It was the growth engine that fueled the building of cities around the world. Steel mills lined the shores of Pittsburgh's three rivers, the Allegheny, the Monongahela, and the Ohio. Smoke spewed up through the smoke stacks and it was often the case that with the sun shining brightly, mid-day in Pittsburgh could resemble midnight. It was an unsustainable environmental nightmare.

From about the middle of the century, city leaders knew that the mills would eventually close and that alternative economic structures needed to be put in place, and they began doing so. When the mills finally closed in the 1980s, jobs were lost, businesses went into bankruptcy, and the great Pittsburgh diaspora took place with people leaving the city in search of new opportunities.

Over these past 30 years, however, Pittsburgh has demonstrated its dogged commitment to build an even better city. Health care and education took the lead at first. Most recently technology and energy leadership have led to a major boom in high tech and natural gas energy companies growing and locating here. Pittsburgh is a city that is determined to move beyond where it was to find its new sense of greatness.

Let's take a look at how we can put the Resilience Continuum to work for ourselves and in our workplaces.

CHAPTER 4

Get Ready and Get Tough

In this chapter, we'll be discussing the preparation phase of the Resilience Continuum™ and its four components: prognostication and creating choices, building grit, creating a mindset in how you approach stressful situations, and finally getting us to stop managing time and begin managing energy.

Predict the Future

Prognostication can be tricky. Even though we want to know what the future holds, most of us are afraid to commit to a path that will drive us toward success. Instead, we merely put some pieces in play and then see how this turns out. This is most evident by how people make committed New Year's resolutions, only to see them disappear by mid-month.

Recently, I was talking with a friend about his son's selection process for choosing a college. Making a sound college selection is an important factor in one's success as an adult. My friend described to me how he and his son scanned campus websites, doing virtual and in-person tours, watched sporting events, talked with other students, checked in with his high school counselor, and spent time dreaming about how exciting his new life would be. My friend and his wife checked the tuition costs and available scholarships and talked to other parents about their experiences. In the end, his son based his decision mostly on a college that "seemed like the right place."

Now I bet that this young man will do just fine at the university he selected and he will have a successful career and happy life. Yet, like so many decisions that we make, we often do not fully explore all the information that is available to us. Could he have spent a weekend or longer on campus? Should he have visited with some professors to find out about possible majors? Should anyone have told him the challenges that he can expect? Understanding the future means that you have as much information as you need to try to create the best outcomes.

Experts tell us that predicting the future is fraught with danger. Steve Ballmer, the former CEO of Microsoft, predicted in 2007 that "there is no chance that the iPhone will gain any significant market share."[xxxiv]

Even people who broke other's predictions didn't believe in making their own. In 1974, Margaret Thatcher, who would become the first woman Prime Minister of the United Kingdom, posited, "It will be years—not in my time—before a woman will become prime minister."[xxxv]

On December 31, 1999, while many of us were celebrating the turn of a new millennium, most tech workers were sitting in front of their computer screens waiting for the end of the world, as the Y2K event was supposed to stop all our computers and along with them power grids, stock markets, and even our clocks. Everyone was certain we would need a serious headache remedy cure for January 1, 2000, but the predicted disasters failed to materialize.

According to researcher Philip Tetlock in his book *Expert Political Judgment*, experts who try to predict the future fail or succeed based on two key approaches they may take in their prognostications. He calls these *Hedgehogs and Foxes.*[xxxvi]

Hedgehogs tend to rely on a single perspective to how they will make their call and are dogmatic about their expectations. Think about political pundits who have a certain agenda they want to promote and interpret everything through that agenda. They tend to be extreme in their predictions.[xxxvii]

Foxes, on the other hand, tend to be more agile in their predictions. They will draw on their life experiences to understand the world along with information from diverse sources. They tend to try out different actions and are willing to admit their mistakes, so they can learn from them. Consider a well-respected scientist who creates a hypothesis to test out a prediction and couches results as probabilities rather than statements of absolutes.

Furthermore, the truth is that we make predictions every single day, but we don't always position them as such:

- Your partner asks you what is on your to-do list today and you think about what you expect that you will get done during your day.
- You prepare an agenda for your meeting with your boss to discuss your current work projects.
- You ask a colleague to go for lunch at a new restaurant because you heard their food is great and you hope that you will not be disappointed.
- Your mother calls you confirming that you'll be coming over to her house this weekend for a family dinner.

Yet when I ask people to guess what their lives will be like outside of the parameters of this week or next, they are at a loss as to what things could be or might be. Taking a shot at where you might be in your career one to three years out seems almost undoable, as is how you think your company might grow over the next year. Yet taking a shot at where or how you want your life to be over the next short-time period can be a great way to avoid future shocks based on a lack of forward thinking. So let's take a moment to have you make a call about your near future.

Given all you know about your current role and the current state of operations for your company, consider all the possibilities as you ponder the following questions:

- Where do you think you will be in your career in the next year?
- Where do you think you will be in three years?
- What do you think your company will be focused on in the next year and in the next three years?
- What will help you the most to achieve your goals and the goals of the organization who employs you?

We sometimes shy away from prognosticating because we see the risk involved in trying to predict what will happen, and most of us tend to be risk averse. We don't want to make a decision that might be wrong, so we wind up making no decision. With no decision, we wind up creating more stress in our lives—due to the fact that by not taking charge of our future, we are giving up our sense of control. Knowing how things we do might turn out helps us moderate the potential of bad or wrong things happening. We are giving ourselves choices that allow us to take a deep breath and acknowledge that we actually have a role in our future. It's not just fate that guides our life.

So what is the key to predictions? We believe it is all about creating choices. For most of us when we consider our options, we tend to look at one or two choices. I call it the "black or white model" of predicting. We tend to look at things in a binary way; it will be either this or that. In most cases, however, the world usually presents us with a color palette to choose from. I like to tell my coaching clients that if they look at the color choices on their computer, they will see that there are well over a million color choices to consider and although there are probably not a million choices we have for the decisions that we have to make, there certainly are more than two.

When it comes to small decisions, such as what you'll enjoy for dinner, you'll probably go with your experience. You love the restaurant's salmon or its Sunday barbeque and you can smell those ribs on the grill. For bigger predictions, give yourself more choices. Take a look at the responses you wrote above and consider whether you went with your first gut responses to your future or your organization's future or whether you considered a range of possibilities. You might have said you would be in the same position a year from now, but what if you opened yourself up to other possibilities? Maybe you'll go back to school for a new degree, or you'll ask for an assignment to a new department to get a feel for different kind of work. Expanding choices makes life more interesting and gives us a challenge that will help us grow.

Predicting the future is nothing more than putting yourself in the driver's seat and deciding this is the route you'll steer—how you want to live your life. By doing so, you'll be identifying and getting ahead of any stress that is out there waiting for you.

Predictions start to build your stress hardiness, which is an important quality of building resilience. We like to emphasize hardiness during the preparatory phase of our resilience work, because the stronger an individual is as they prepare for stressful times, the better they will be able to handle stress when it comes their way. Although hardiness is often described as the ability to endure difficult times, we see hardiness as being the commitment an individual shows toward building up their strength and endurance in the face of anticipatory stressful conditions. We build hardiness in any number of ways that promote discipline and effort. By demonstrating patience in reading and researching all the available information on a topic to become a subject matter expert in your field, you gain not only knowledge but also confidence in your ability to discuss the topic. Encouraging your child to stick with a tough homework assignment to completion shows him or her that stick-to-it-iveness is a value worth possessing.

Get Gritty

The past few Boston Marathons may have been some of the most important in the race's storied history given the tragedy of the 2013 terrorist event. "Boston Strong," as it has become known, celebrated the fortitude and courage of that city by running the event without pause, setting an example of how Boston and our country would not be cowered by extremists. The city of Boston, birthplace of our nation, doesn't cower very easily. The people of Boston showed their grit in 2013.

In 1967, the race experienced another kind of grittiness that also changed it forever.

Katherine Switzer was a young journalist student at Syracuse University. She loved to run and unofficially joined the men's cross country-running team so that she could get miles in with other runners. During her training that took place during snowy New England days, she met a veteran runner of 15 Boston Marathons, Arnie Biggs, who regaled her with stories of the race. Soon, she caught the bug and knew she wanted to run the Marathon. There was just one problem, however: Women were not allowed to run the Boston Marathon.

Three weeks before the race in early April, she demonstrated to herself and Arnie that she could completed the race by running the full 26 miles in practice. She was physically ready to go but didn't know what might confront her as the first woman to ever officially run the race.

She registered as K.V. Switzer and was joined by Arnie and her boyfriend, Tom Miller, who was a former All-American football player.

Conditions on race day were like many of her training days, snowy and cold. As the race started, many of her fellow racers welcomed her as the first woman to the Boston Marathon. Around mile four, a media truck caught up to her and started taking pictures. A few minutes later, however, the race coordinator, Jock Semple, jumped onto the racecourse and attempted to pull her down while screaming at her, "Get out of my race and give me those numbers." He might have succeeded if Katherine's boyfriend Tom hadn't thrown a mean body block to get Jock off Katherine's back!

She was shaken up and before she could collect herself, the media truck returned with reporters showering her with questions about "What is she trying to prove? When would you give up?" Additionally, another vehicle came along with Jock, who was now threatening her that she was in "big trouble."

Katherine just put her head down and kept running her race. Although she had been drained of energy due in large part to these "extracurricular" activities, she turned to her coach and told him that now she *had* to finish just to show everyone that a woman could complete the race, even if she had to do so on her hands and knees.

As she approached the famous Heartbreak Hill, she found herself getting mad about how women were restricted from sports. Blisters started forming on her feet. She endured the pain telling herself that this race had become bigger than just a marathon run.

Four hours and 20 minutes after starting the race, Switzer finished and broke a barrier that went beyond running a race. As her father had told her a few weeks before the run, "Aw, hell, kid, you can do it. You're tough, you've trained, you'll do great."

And she did.[xxxviii]

Psychologist Angela Duckworth has been studying grit for the past dozen years and has identified two major ways that grit is an important component of resilience.

First, grit is about how one deals with adversity and challenges and whether one persists in overcoming these difficulties. It is the classic idea of what we think about resilience that it is the ability to persist and bounce back from struggles. Many people face these situations in office settings every day.

Duckworth also identified another aspect of grit that has to do with having a focused long-held belief or passion. These may be represented by your natural strengths or interests that create an achievement orientation for you. With that kind of long-term belief in place for oneself, the opportunity for success and achievement has a greater chance for success. (This is also a common workplace phenomenon with top performers.)

Using these two broad measures of grit, she surveyed new students at West Point who were enrolled in a summer training program. This program which gave these new cadets a taste of what their academic experiences would be at the Academy, was designed to help weed out students who would not find the West Point experience to their liking.

Her concept of grit was a better determinant of which students would persist in the program than was the rigorous "Whole Candidate Score" that is used by the Army for admission.[xxxix]

Grit is important for us because it helps to build our fortitude and the stick-to-it-iveness that we need to succeed when things get tough. It is represented by a determination and commitment.

In a recent phone call, the head of an architectural firm specifically brought up the topic of grit, which he saw as a vitally important component of his firm's culture. His organization's cultural grit meant that they had to endure challenging times during their early growth period. It seemed like there were always difficulties in his business. Recently, he had to fire three people who were not good fits for his company, and the firm had lost several recent bids on projects that he thought they would win. Furthermore, he didn't feel his team was working in as coordinated a manner as possible, which affected their productivity and, ultimately, their success.

When I asked how he was going to address this, his voice changed on the phone. It was almost I could see him sitting up in his chair. His response was clear. "Just like we always do when we've missed the mark on anything, we'll pick ourselves up, refocus our efforts, and follow our plan. I'm not sure I know anything else to do."

His words represent the key elements of grit. Anyone can develop and improve on the way build the storehouse of energy needed when adversity comes their way.

1. **Embrace failure**: We've been taught to fear and avoid failure. Failing is bad and you should work to never fail. This may sound like a great idea but it's obviously very unreasonable and unrealistic. Failure is

inevitable. Although it may be difficult to accept that it comes our way, changing our perception of how we deal with failure helps us see that it is not life- or world-changing and that, in fact, we get another opportunity tomorrow. Taking time to learn from that mistake is the key turnaround for growing from failures. Start small to understand and to embrace your failures. You'll probably take your failure personally, but try looking at it objectively and consider that the failure was not all your fault.

2. **Persistence:** I like to say that getting my PhD is less a hallmark of intelligence and more about persistence. I have plenty of friends and colleagues who would agree with me regarding my intelligence. Persistence is about staying with a task that you believe is important. You already possess the persistence quality in activities that you enjoy. ("Eighty percent of success is showing up."—Woody Allen.[xl]) For example, if you are a gear head and love working on cars, you have no problem spending your weekend at car shows and then playing around with your 1965 Chevy convertible. You'll stay with that activity all day long.

Of course, being persistent with something we love is a bit different than persisting with something that is challenging or difficult for us, but once again reducing it to small parts can help us translate our skill with positive persistence. Time and focus are the keys to developing greater persistence, and you can experiment with those factors. One of my clients was working on a long and arduous technical manual for her company when she told me that she committed to working on it in 45-minute blocks of time that she built into her morning and afternoon work. It seemed that three-quarters of an hour was about all she could take, but it was enough to allow her to complete the task within the allocated time.

3. **Focused passions:** This is one of Angela Duckworth's key definitions of grit.[xli] Having a long-held belief or value builds a path for your life that keeps a focus on importance. It may relate to family or your career. It could be as a result of a long-time drive that you possess or it could be tied to an event that occurred to you as an adult.

When Candy Lightner's daughter was killed by a repeat drunk driver, she knew she had to do something more than just grieve her loss. She mobilized her energy and founded MADD, Mothers Against Drunk Drivers, with a mission to change the laws across the country so that drunk drivers could not kill other young people. Her campaign succeeded in not just changing the laws, but also changing our cultural thinking about drinking and driving. Hopefully, developing your passion will come through meaningful experiences and not tragedy.

4. **Be open to shifting possibilities:** As we've discussed, resilience to challenging events is more than a personal quality. It is also a cultural quality. When it comes to thinking outside the box, no culture may be better than the Dutch in terms of how they've dealt with flood management.

   Almost all of Holland is within one yard above sea level, so for all its history it has dealt with flooding. We know about the Dutch systems of dikes and dams, that kept the water at bay for hundreds of years, but today their approach is different. It is not about keeping the water out *but instead recognizing that they can't stop the water and discovering ways to work with the water when it rises.* Their current plan is to build wide trenches in several cities. They will use the dugout land to raise the level of surrounding areas to allow for new housing and offices. The trenched areas will become parks during periods of low water and rivers and lakes during periods of high water. Interestingly, many people in the local community were initially angered by this action. They believed Holland's long-held theory that keeping water out was the best way to manage their flooding issues, but persistent discussion and communication paved the way for new ideas

Grit is an important quality in building strengths that we can rely on when times get tough. Our natural tendency is to want to confront the challenges we face immediately, but making sure we've built the behaviors to support the skill will improve our ability to succeed.

Creating Mindset

I am often asked, "What is the one thing that I can do to improve how I deal with stress?" Everyone wants to know what is the magic bullet that will help him or her gain some control over his or her stress levels.

If you only have time to do one thing, this section is for you. And that one thing would be how you think about the stress in your life.

How we think about the stress in our lives comprises our "mindset" about stress. "Mindset" is the collection of thoughts, ideas, and beliefs that directly impact the behaviors we manifest in dealing with stress. As we've noted, the stress management model has taught us that we should view ourselves as incapable of dealing effectively with our stress.

An amazing example of our negative mindset about stress is tied to a research project that tracked 30,000 Americans over an eight-year period. Abiola Keller and colleagues from the University of Wisconsin and the National Cancer Institute examined data from the National Health Interview Survey from 1998 and compared it to data from the National Death Index in 2006. Among the items that people were asked about were ones about perceived level of stress in life along with whether or not they viewed stress in general as harmful to their health. The researchers found an increased risk of premature death by 43% among those people who reported a high level of stress and thought that stress was a negative in their lives. The researchers recognized that although these statistics point to the power of negative thinking, they also acknowledged that having a more positive and resilient attitude toward stress could work to decrease its impact on our health.[xlii]

How we perceive and think about the stress in our life is what comprises our mindset about it. Most of us were taught (in our stress management classes) that the only reactions to stress are a "fight or flight" response in which we are only able to confront the stress or run from it. Although that is true from a purely physiological and body response perspective, the fact that we have a mind that is able to perceive and consider how we want to deal with stress, provides us with additional choices in how we see and experience our stress.

Perceptions represent a way that we often frame our own minds around stressful situations. If we see an upcoming stressful situation as a do-able challenge, then we can see ourselves as possessing the resources to adequately deal with that situation. If we view the same situation as something for which we do not have the requisite skills, then we see the stressor as a threat. Distinctions between how we approach these two mindsets are represented in Table 4.1.

However, sometimes our own perceptions of what is a challenge and what is a threat may be misperceived.

Case Study

In a recent consulting assignment, I was working with the senior vice president of operations and his direct report, the director of a specific division that was having operational difficulties. When I met with the division director, she shared her excitement about the project objectives that would help the operating team work together in a more coordinated fashion. The team had missed their production levels and there was a fair amount of infighting going on between work groups. She saw the project as vitally important and believed that her team would step up to the plate and do what they needed to do to improve the facility once the project objectives were embraced.

The team member who was overseeing the facility had a totally different view of the project. He perceived it as dangerous, in that it forced people to work as a team when they didn't have the skills or interest in working together and that, in turn, would only yield an angry workforce. And an angry workforce would make more production errors. He didn't want to move ahead on the project, thinking it was better to do nothing than risk creating more divisiveness.

Was this project a challenge for the operating team? Or a threat?

Table 4.1

Challenge Condition	Threat Condition
• I have the skills for this	• This seems overwhelming
• I am going all out to win	• Maybe I can just not lose too badly
• I am going to learn from this experience	• I hope I don't screw up too bad
• I feel energized by this situation	• I feel exhausted just thinking about this situation
• Bring it on	• Do I have to do this?

Many of us fall victim to experiencing a negative perspective on a regular basis. The negativity bias, which has its origins as a protective biological factor going back to our early ancestors ("I better watch my back while I'm out hunting for food to make sure that the saber tooth tiger is not hunting me"), continues to influence our thinking. Simply put, when we think the worst will happen rather than the best, we are falling prey to the negativity bias. Consider how you respond to either a negative or a positive situation in your life. When the negative situation happens, you may say, "I expected that to happen," or, "These kinds of crummy things always affect me." When a positive happens, you may think, "Boy, am I lucky. These kinds of things never happen for me." We tend to expect negatives and discount positives.

In situations where we manifest the negativity bias, we see the world or situations as more threatening and dangerous, rather than seeing challenges that can be interesting and perhaps even exciting.

What if we turn the table on the negativity bias and actively create a perception that stress is not bad, but instead is something good. The idea that stress is good for us derives from the notion that by challenging ourselves we create opportunities for growth and success.

Recently a young client of mine received word that she was being promoted to her boss's position as he went off to a new job himself. After I sent her a congratulatory e-mail, she sent me back the following response, "Thanks! To be honest I am still quite shocked, nervous, and overwhelmed but up for the challenge."

Creating a *positive stress mindset* takes some time and an openness to see the world a bit differently. Researcher and professor Carol Dweck at Stanford University has identified that each of us approach learning in one of two ways. People with a fixed mindset tend to see their world as static and don't believe that change happens very easily. Fixed mindsetters believe that their world is carved in stone, that they have to make the best of what they have, and that there is little opportunity for growth. People with a growth mindset see the world in a different way. They believe that their inherent talents are meant to be stepping stones that will help them achieve and grow more. They are learners and are constantly striving to improve on their capabilities and performance.[xliii]

If you have a growth mindset and want to begin to see how you can approach your stress differently, creating an affirming mindset will help you set the stage for decreased stress and more resilience. There are any numbers of strategies you can use to change how you perceive the stress in your life. Additionally, you can build this capacity on the front end during the preparation phase of the Resilience Continuum, so that you get a jump on any predictable or even unpredicted challenges. Some of the strategies you can try:

1. **Change your self-talk:** When something good happens, don't tell yourself you are lucky; tell yourself you are good. When something bad happens, don't make full attribution to your effort; spread the responsibility around.

2. **Don't merely focus on failed efforts**, but move to the next outcome that you want. Dweck found that students with fixed mindsets wanted to know how they did on school tests, whereas students with growth mindsets asked what they could do to improve.[xliv] Careful analysis means that you consider what you did poorly, what you did well, and exactly how you will do things differently in the future.

3. **Experience something new.** This may be travel or volunteer work or even reading a non-fiction book if you've always been a fiction reader. Doing something new helps create new neural pathways and teaches you something you did not know before. It's highly possible that the new learning opens up a new perspective for you.

4. **Stop telling yourself that stress is bad.** This is a big one for us. We see people walking around their office every day complaining about the stress level in their job. "It's so stressful here," has become a meme in many workplaces. As we saw in the research study cited above, believing that stress is a negative contributes to increased mortality. We wouldn't be surprised if it also contributes to hating our work. Instead, if you are having a really tough day, try telling yourself, "Today is a challenging day, but I am doing okay."

5. **Take on a challenging assignment at work.** Many people are content to just do their job every day and some of them do that for 25, 30, or even 40 years. Imagine how much they are missing from not pushing their own learning to see what they can achieve. It may seem scary to ask to do more work, but most probably you'll do very well, develop a new skill set, or even become a thought leader in your organization, and you will be pleasantly surprised by your new-found success. Remember, some things can't be taught, they can only be learned.

Events, even stressful events are neutral by nature. They just occur. How we perceive, judge, and experience them is what creates the stress in our bodies. How you approach stressful situations in your mind (your mindset) may be the closest to a magic bullet for addressing stress successfully. A positive stress mindset builds fortitude or hardiness in the face of challenges. And this mindset we want to build begins by being open to the idea that stress is not the enemy but is really your friend. Embracing it rather than fighting it will create a great deal more ease and resilience in your life.

Your Most Precious Resource

There are only 24 hours, 1,440 minutes, or 86,400 seconds in a day. That is it. When that second hand ticks to the next second, that prior second is lost. There is no more and no less. We can't increase that time and although we think we manage time, we don't do any better at that than we do with stress. It's another one of those imperatives.

The truth is that time manages us better than we think we manage it. Our effort to address time is determined by how we spend it on our different activities. Those activities that we spend more time on are our *de facto* priorities. Those we spend less time on become our less important priorities. Say, for example, that you are planning to go to the gym to work out, but instead you get enthralled with your friend's vacation pictures on Facebook. You wind up Facebooking instead of working out, which is fine. Oftentimes, folks will get upset and stressed out later about the choice they made. I would encourage a more accepting and forgiving approach to time. No need to feel bad. At that moment, being on Facebook was more important to you than exercising.

Time is really about priorities. We do *have* time, 24 hours daily, and time to decide how to apply it. "I don't have time for my daughter's soccer match" means you've decided not to go (perhaps with good reason, perhaps not), but that excuse is faulty because you have the time, you've just decided that it is not the priority for you that day.

Most of us spend as much time trying to manage time as we do actually spending time doing things. We make lists, we revise our Outlook calendar, we write notes to ourselves, make meeting requests, fill in our manual date book. If you are like me, I'll even tell Siri to make an appointment for later in the day to remind me to make an appointment with someone! Our effort to manage time is probably doomed to fail due to the limited and finite nature of this commodity and the vast number of distractions that exist in our lives.

We may want to ditch time and instead focus on something we can control such as our own personal energy.

Energy is the ability to get work done. Energy exists in different forms. One type of energy happens when your work is going well and you are feeling positive about your projects. You feel pumped, excited, and strong. Your smile and "can do" encourages everyone around you. You are an energy creator. Alternatively, there may be somebody at your workplace who is an energy drainer. Perhaps he or she is the person who is always complaining and whining and not getting things done. They suck the energy right out of the room and after spending time with them you may feel like you need a nap.

Energy management is particularly important during this preparation phase of the Resilience Continuum, because there are several ways you can approach it. One approach relates to the amount of energy available to spend during the day. Energy management, in this instance, has to do with the amount and quality of rest you've had, how you build endurance, and how effective your energy management strategies are during the day.

A second approach is about how you create or build your energy storehouse or robustness. This has more to do with how you approach your own health and wellness. Exercise is a good example. Some people who exercise at the end of the day may say that their exercise routine helps to work off their stress, whereas the people who exercise in the morning often say that their exercise gives them strength for the day. Nutrition is another example. Eat a heavy starch-filled lunch and you'll be struggling to keep your eyes open until your system works that off. Eat a protein-rich lunch and you'll probably be more focused on your afternoon tasks. Recognizing how your body works and making the choices that fit you means that you can endure more challenges and difficulties and have the storehouse of liveliness to get through your more difficult stressors.

We have within our daily capacity only so much energy that we can expend. You wake up in the morning and may feel rested. By the end of the day, you are fatigued. What happens during the day is the difference between that energy potential in the morning and the energy exhaustion at the end of the night. Restoring our energy relates to the quality of our sleep and understanding your personal sleep requirements (not what they say on Yahoo news) is your key to rebuilding your energy storehouse overnight.

Even if you've had a bad night's sleep, it is possible to create restorative energy during the day. Remember when you were a kindergartner and you were able to put your head on your desk and rest. Not such a bad idea. Recovering energy during the day is a doable task. My wife, Sheila, takes Zumba classes and tells me that after moving non-stop for 60 minutes, she feels more energized than she did before her class. She likes to say, "Dancing doesn't take energy; it makes energy."

Let's examine some factors around personal energy. First of all, everybody's energy timing is different. In my house, I am an early riser usually getting up around 5 a.m. I take an early morning walk and am ready to start my day writing or preparing for clients by 7 a.m. As the day progresses, my energy begins to dwindle and by the evening, I'm pretty pooped. My wife, on the other hand, is a slow starter in the morning but gets focused as the day goes on. She is likely to stay up writing a blog post or article long after I've gone to bed at 9:30 or 10 p.m. Energy levels are different for each individual. We can use an energy tracker to monitor how energy ebbs and flows during the day (Figure 4.1).

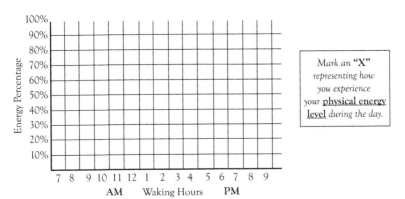

Figure 4.1 Energy Level Tracker: Physical Energy

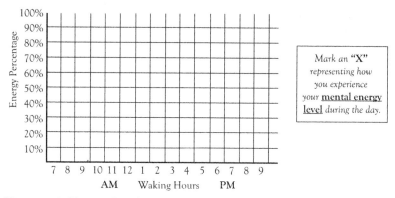

Mark an "X"
representing how
you experience
your **mental energy**
level *during the day.*

Figure 4.2 Energy Level Tracker: Mental Energy

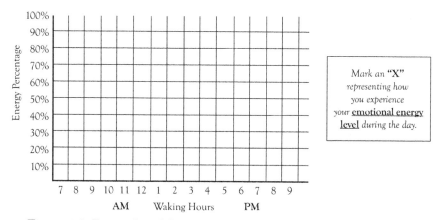

Mark an "X"
representing how
you experience
your **emotional energy**
level *during the day.*

Figure 4.3 Energy Level Tracker: Emotional Energy

To use this tracker, merely record your perception of how much available energy you have each hour of the day. Most people will use the tracker to record their physical energy levels, but you can also use this to track your mental or emotional level. You will want to record five days of data, including a weekend day, so that you can get a good read on how your energy levels run during the week.

The second element or key idea about personal energy is that all hours are *not* created equal. Building on idea one, you may know that you are a more creative thinker in the morning and that by mid-afternoon you're better off completing expense reports rather than drafting an operational plan, since your creative juices are shot. On the other hand, it may be better for you right after lunch to do something that involves filling out mundane paperwork, because you have to try to work off that after-lunch lethargy. Better to do that than to schedule a meeting with your boss where you may find yourself drifting off to nap. Paying attention to how your energy shifts during the day is really important, and this is one of the ideas that is missed by many time management people. For them, all hours are created equal, but for personal energy people, all hours are created differently.

When do you do your best work? What kind of work are you doing during that part of the day?

When do you do your worst work? What kind of work should you be doing during this time of the day?

The third key idea in energy management I alluded to a little bit earlier when I talked about my wife's Zumba class. You can create more energy by doing things that you find fun and enjoyable, including in the workplace. Now, we are not going to have the time during the day to do everything that we find enjoyable and fun, but we want to make sure that we build in things during our day that are rewarding to us. That will give you more energy.

I worked with a senior leader who found his energy levels draining during his meeting days, as if someone had pulled the plug on his own energy storehouse. He recognized that there were two things that were missing from his workday.

First was time for quiet reflection, when he could have built in structured minutes to think about the big picture and to give his mind a break from the daily routine of problem solving and issues management. The second was time to meet and talk with his line staff to see what he could learn from them. He took a deliberate approach of asking his staff, "What are you working on that is exciting to you? What are you working on that is frustrating to you?"

As we worked out a plan, he decided to put these two practices on his calendar several times a week. He told his assistant that these were sacred times that he did not want to be disturbed. Today, he reports that when he is able to hold that time in place, he feels enlivened and more productive. Plus, it helps his team to see that he is committed to being with them.

According to William Anthony, a researcher at Boston University, napping has a powerful effect on physical and mental restoration, with gains being made even with a 15-minute power nap. His survey research indicated that over 70 percent of those surveyed reported that they've napped on the job. Companies such as British Airways and Union Pacific Railway encourage their pilots and conductors to take 30-minute naps with proper safety procedures in place. Of course, if your workplace does not support this kind of action, you can at least know that you can always go to the "rest room" for a little quiet time.

The fifth and final key to personal energy management is about using our personal energy dashboard. Our car's console has a fuel and temperature gauge, speedometer, and odometer that keep us informed about our car's performance. Today's advanced vehicles use state-of-the-art computer sensors to manage the car's temperature, alert us to when we are getting too close to another car when parking, and are even able to prepare our car to slow down in traffic due to radar housed in the front grill. What if we can begin to apply technology for preparing and tracking our stress levels, so that we are able to better understand how our body is preparing and reacting to a particular stress, providing us with an opportunity to be

Digression: Be aware that the job requirements for energy should at least roughly match your personal "battery." If you put a small battery into a huge energy role, such as a nurse, for example, you will see errors of commission in terms of doctors' orders and administering drugs.

If you put a strong battery in a low-energy job, such as a TSA screener, you will see errors of omission as boredom and tedium dull one's senses.

We really don't want exceptionally low-key nurses, nor people on the TSA monitors at airports who have high energy and are bored looking at all those bags all day long.

mindful about how we choose to respond? Energy trackers, like the Apple Watch and Fitbit, are leading the way in helping us gain insight into our own energy management.

Our personal energy is our most valuable commodity. Some people think that time is the most precious factor in our lives, but it is actually energy, because we can control our energy while we can't control time. How we use our energy determines our success, our victories, and perhaps even our happiness.

CHAPTER 5

Navigating the Waters

In this chapter, we'll examine the second aspect of the *Resilience Continuum,* addressing stress in real time. We'll explore why this is such a challenging skill to develop, why some people do it well, and how each of us can use the inherent knowledge that exists within biology to create more grace in pressure-filled situations.

The most challenging aspect of being stress resilient is dealing with stress in real time. When confronted by a difficult or challenging situation, we lose control, and we become lost in our biological response. That may be fine in cases of real emergencies, but many of our evoked stress reactions are not life or death, even if we sometimes make ourselves seem like they are.

Despite our difficulty in dealing with these kinds of nonemergency situations, the reasons for it are perfectly predictable. It's caused by how our primitive or mammalian brain deals with crises. This part of our brain, also known as our limbic system, deals with crises as if our very existence is at risk, causing us to break into the flight, fight, or freeze response, which is that overwhelming feeling you get when your body responds to a real or merely perceived threat. This biological response is great if we are trying to avoid a traffic accident but doesn't work very well when our boss stops in and throws a "due tomorrow" project on our desk. If we are going to be stress resilient, we want to be able to deal with these kinds of challenges with more ease, comfort, and grace at the moment they occur.

Think about people who handle crises effectively in real time. I often view professional athletes, as they respond to real live situations as they happen on the playing field, as a great example of people who are cool under pressure. I think it's one of the reasons that watching sports is so popular. We want to see how these athletes perform under real-time pressure, and there is much we can learn from people who perform well in such difficult, stressful situations.

Successful athletes keep themselves cool and handle the pressure of the game flawlessly. NBA basketball star Steph Curry looks almost lazy as he tosses in a 3 point shot at the buzzer while fans are up screaming and exhausting themselves from the anxiety they are experiencing as they watch their beloved team run up and down the court. What is the secret of cool that those guys know and that we all want to possess?

Let's examine how to maintain that cool in your world and offer suggestions for you to be successful on your field of play.

Stress in Real Time

Select any event:

- You are getting ready for work and your 13-year-old son tells you he is feeling sick and does not want to go to school. He was fine last night and now you have to evaluate his health, but you also have to leave for work NOW!
- Your boss calls you and tells you to get to his office right away. There is a problem!
- You get a call from your father telling you that your mother has to go to the oncologist's office for an evaluation for breast cancer. Her primary doctor is very concerned.
- Your team comes into your office and is frantic about a phone call from a customer telling them that she is taking her business somewhere else.

Just writing these possible events gets me nervous and they are all hypothetical. Yet that is how the stress reaction works on us biologically, and this is the main reason that we cannot manage stress. When we have a situation that creates a stressful experience for us, our bodies are going to release their stress hormones and we are going to react accordingly.

This aspect of stress, navigating in real time while it is actually happening, is the most difficult aspect of addressing the stress in our life. It is one in which being resilient can help us.

The resilience approach helps us to deal with stress in real time, because we soon recognize that stress is something that is going to happen to us, and it provides us tools that allow us to step back, recognize that we are in a stressful situation, and know that we can moderate, mitigate, or even embrace the challenge presented by the stress reaction.

Let's examine how we typically react to some of the situations we described above.

In the first situation, you are on an internal time schedule. It is 7 a.m. and you know that you have to leave the house by 7.15 a.m. in order to give yourself the 45 minutes you need to get to work, so that you have 30 minutes to prepare for that presentation to your senior leaders. Your 13-year old is still in bed complaining about not feeling well and not wanting to go to school. You are torn between needing to leave and concern for your son's health. Your mind is working double time to figure out how you can take the extra 15 minutes to evaluate your son's condition and still make it to work in time. You head is pounding and your stomach is churning as you keep looking at your watch to figure out what to do. You default to work, tell him to stay home and out of trouble, and off you go to work. Crisis averted.

The second situation has the element of surprise to it. It generates an unanticipated anxiety that creates a kind of fear factor that has you breathing deeply as you head over to your boss's office, wondering exactly what the problem might be about. To make matters worse, by not knowing the specifics, you'll have the double trouble of carrying your anxiety in to the meeting with you and then having to think on your feet about addressing a problem that you'll have no time to prepare to discuss! Physically, your heart is racing and even your efforts to breathe deeply seem to fall miserably short. You head up to your boss's office trying not to hold your breath.

The third situation feels like a punch in the gut. People usually have several different reactions to this situation. The first is fear. Fear for your mom and what this diagnosis might be about. Fear for your dad since you know he doesn't handle these things too well, and fear for yourself as you realize your family life may be getting ready to go topsy-turvy. The second reaction people have is to jump into problem-solving mode. Does mom have the capable most oncologist? What are the best treatment options? Should I call my friend's ex-husband who works at that major cancer treatment center? At a physical level, we might feel like the wind has been knocked out of us but our mind starts to give us some ideas on how to react. The question that stews in our belly…what should I do? Support mom and dad or try to solve the problem.

The final situation may also provide you with different reactions, as your body and mind play a game of tag team deciding how you want to respond to the situation. Privately, you may have an "Oh no!" reaction to the news that a current customer is taking the business somewhere else. Your brow starts to sweat and your anxiety increases as you try to figure out what could have happened that prompted such a good customer to leave. You are also, however, your team's leader. In that role, you want to keep things calm, so that your team sees you as being able to address the challenge facing them. You move, first, to "I have to make sure I understand the issue at hand," while working to manage the sense of panic that you see strewn across the faces of your team members. You are the boss and they are all looking to you for leadership.

Although each of these situations is different, some related to work and some to home, there are obviously common themes that occur when we are in the teeth of a stressful situation. What do we see as the commonalities?

1. **There is a body reaction to all these events**. Our body reacts to these and other events that we perceive as stress, releasing the stress hormones of adrenaline and cortisol to create the reactions we feel when stressed. Adrenaline creates the immediate reaction we experience. It is what gets our heart pumping, our breathing quicker, and our muscles tenser. We are ready for action. Cortisol takes a few minutes to kick in and its primary job is to regulate certain body processes that aren't necessary for survival when we are in the crisis mode, such as digestion and libido. Under chronic stress conditions in which our bodies maintain a state of chronic stress, cortisol is continuously released ultimately suppressing our immune system. While our body releases cortisol to mediate the stress situation, as soon as the crisis abates, our nervous system releases acetylcholine that counters the effects of cortisol and allows our body to return to a calmer state. Using our built-in resilience systems helps us return to a calm and even keeled position. Our biology strives to create resilience.

2. At the same time that our body is reacting to these events, **the thinking brain kicks into action to help address these challenges posed above**. Problem solving, conflict management, judgment, and decision-making are all aspects of how our mind uses its hard-wired drive to seek solutions. In some instances, we may make sound, well-informed decisions such as in the last scenario, where a loss of business requires careful thought. Other situations, like when your kid is ill and opting out of school, may be related to expediency. Still others, such as when your boss calls you up to her office, leave you hanging, just doing your best to predict and hope that you have enough facts to address her concerns. All these efforts are designed to help dial down the intense level of stress we are physically experiencing.

3. **We drive toward solutions**. Even in the face of the most intense stress situations, we are constantly working toward mitigating the problem, seeking an explanation and gaining a resolution. Our bodies are responding to the event in a way that seems to cause us distress, but is actually working to solve the problem quickly and efficiently.

That's because our bodies have an innate capacity for good decision making, which we might call wisdom.

Building Body Wisdom

Navigating our stress reaction in real time is one tough task. Our bodies are programmed to respond to emergencies in a set pattern that has been biologically programmed for thousands of years. It usually feels as if we are just along for the ride. That is another reason why the stress management model has been so prominent for us. It seems as if there is nothing we can do to deal with our stress reaction.

Let's begin this little journey by quickly looking at a simple perspective of how our brains operate, since it is in our brains that our stress challenges begin. Our brain is actually composed of three different components, each of which plays a variety of different functions for us.

The so-called oldest or "reptilian" part of our brain is located deep within our head. This part of our brain controls our most basic and vital functions, such as breathing, heart rate, blood pressure, and other automatic aspects of our body (such as digestion). It also serves as a kind of watchdog so that, for example, if we are sleeping and a noise occurs in our home, this part of our brain will wake us and alert us to check to make sure there is no danger. This brain operates automatically for us, so we do not have to think about these activities at all.

Our second brain is known as the *mammalian* or *limbic brain*, and it is the emotional center of our lives. It is this part of our brain that is responsible for the fight, flight, or freeze response that we typically associate with the stress reaction. The limbic system is what makes it impossible for us to "manage stress," in that this part of our brain responds automatically to stress situations and doesn't ever bother to ask us if we want to get involved in that event. This part of the brain is made up of a number or important brain structures such as the hypothalamus, hippocampus, and amygdala that are responsible for sending nerve impulses to different parts of the body to respond to stress situations. They may send an order to the adrenal glands to release adrenalin and cortisol, both of which help us respond to the emergency we are facing.

Our cerebral cortex, which is located on the outer surface of our brain, is our *thinking brain*. It is responsible for higher-ordered activities such as our use of language, problem solving, memory, and consciousness. The cortex, especially our prefrontal cortex, allows us to understand, analyze, and think through complex problems. Although our limbic system is working overtime to try to manage the crisis and stress we are facing, there lies within our neocortex the opportunity to change the way we address our stress by building our resilience, so that we are not trying to manage stress *but instead are using our stress for growth.*

You may reasonably ask yourself how your brain responds to stress situations. Do you jump into the fight, flight, or freeze response that would suggest your limbic system runs the show? Or, are you able to let the stress response move through you and then consider what actions you want to take? We could call this your stress "style," as this is your common response to a challenging situation. It requires an ability to notice how you respond to different situations. We usually operate on autopilot around these issues, so the first step is to begin by noticing, even after the fact, how you reacted in stressful situation. Don't worry about finding big situations to notice. There are always plenty of everyday, run-of-the-mill stress experiences that you can begin observing.

My personal favorite is noticing how I behave on the highway. These days, construction is happening all over the highways and it leads to massive backups and delays. Having grown up and learned my driving in New York City, I tend to be something of an assertive driver (my wife might say a bit aggressive, but we'll leave that interpretation for another time). I'll usually bob and weave in traffic, looking for the opportunity to pick up a faster lane here or going back to the lane in which I started, because I see fewer red lights down that side of the road. I'll drive to a merge point in construction and will do more than just turn on my directional signal, I'll actually roll down my window, lean out and ask the driver who I want to merge in front of if I can enter at this point. I am rarely turned down. I'm in my fight response to the stress of highway driving these days and I can feel it when my heart races faster and my aggravation level gets higher when I choose a wrong lane.

A second option is when I take time to notice my response and decide to back off and dial down that action. I stay in my lane, let other drivers get in the lane in front of me, turn on my radio to music instead of more bad news, and just decide that I'll get to my destination when I get there. It's Margaritaville without the Margarita. I'm embracing the stress of the situation and deciding that I am not going to let it get to me. I am more in a relaxation mode and I've *decided* that I can override my normal stress reaction.

Dr. Dan Siegel is a professor of psychiatry at UCLA who has studied brain functioning for over 30 years. Dr. Siegel has identified that the prefrontal cortex of our brain, the most advanced portion of our brain, is responsible for, among other activities, nine core functions that can help regulate the stress reaction and create a more resilient approach in stress situations. His work, known as interpersonal neurobiology, attempts to link how the brain develops and grows in relationship to how we relate to one another.[xlv]

This includes:

1. **An ability to stay calm in stressful situations**. Consider how professional athletes are able to regulate their emotions in tense game situations, or think of my choice to not get sucked into traffic stress. Think about the sales professional who turns a complaint into an even larger sale.

2. **Being attuned to what others are experiencing,** so that you are not caught up in your own stress. Think about the boss needing to support his team worried about that lost contract. She can't be overly focused on her fears, as she needs to use the entire team to solve this problem.

3. **Modulating the fear response.** The negativity bias seems to force us to choose only bad options. The prefrontal cortex can help us moderate the fear we often fear. Most situations are not really dangerous, and using our advanced brain to get a realistic picture of situations can only help us. The prospective buyer is not shooting at us.

4. **Understanding ourselves.** Self-awareness means that you know what actions you may take in any particular situation. You are predictable to yourself and with that ability you can begin to consider how you may want to change how you address stress situations. Many people visualize the coming meeting or event or speech.

5. **Being empathetic.** Understanding others provides you a strategic advantage in working and being with others. Developing this unique ability to know how another person is feeling means that you can have stunning insight into how others may react, allowing you to address and mitigate how others manage their stress before it gets to you. *Sympathy* means that you feel what the other person is feeling, but *empathy* means that you understand what the other person is feeling.

6. **Having response flexibility.** We've discussed expanding our choice palette in our discussion around predicting. It applies again here in navigating real time stress. Engaging our prefrontal cortex helps increase the choices we have, and with it the potential to increase outcomes that provide greater chances for success.

7. **Dealing effectively with your emotions.** Do you ever feel like your emotions are getting the better of you? Learning how to regulate your emotions in different situations is a way that our brain helps us to stay in control. Taking a deep breath allows us to reboot our emotional senses.

8. **Using your intuition.** Our "gut" instincts are smart. Think back to times when you had a hunch about something. These instincts are usually physiological feelings we have in our body that are then

run up to our prefrontal cortex for interpretation and action. For example, have you ever felt that something was "over your head" or that you are "warming up to a new colleague"? We use language to interpret and translate these feelings that often have important messages for us.

9. **Morality**. When we gain better control over our own actions and response to challenging situations, Dr. Siegel suggests that we also begin to take on a larger social responsibility.[xlvi] We see our connection to the bigger world and we want to help whether it is being a better listener to a friend in need or donating time at your neighborhood food bank. Capitalism, our economic system itself, is based on the moral premise that one party will provide something of a certain quality in a certain amount at a certain time in return for agreed upon compensation. Right now, this system seems to be under some duress as ideas of economic inequality are creating some social unrest.

We'll discuss strategies for building capabilities a bit later in this chapter, but for now what is important to remember is that our thinking brain can be engaged to help us address challenging situations when they occur in real time so that we don't have to default to our mammalian brain's automatic response.

Building body wisdom is more, however, than just using the power of our prefrontal cortex to help us navigate challenges and stress in real time. We also have to use the rest the resources of our body. Turns out our bodies have a number of different nervous systems that provide us with information that can be understood and used by the prefrontal cortex to make decisions to help us address our daily challenges.

The response our body has to stress and its release of the stress hormones such as adrenaline and cortisol is known as the *sympathetic nervous system*. Its counterpart is called the *parasympathetic nervous system*, and among its hormones are acetylcholine and oxytocin, both of which help relax the body. Oxytocin, a recently discovered hormone, has been nicknamed the "cuddle hormone," as it is involved in helping bond relationships. Oxytocin has been noted to be at higher levels in people during the early stages of relationships, as well as for moms during and after their labor delivery. Part of the benefit of giving and getting a hug when we're down may be that a little bit of oxytocin is released, helping us to feel better through our connection with others.

Ever have the feeling of "butterflies in your stomach?" Or "having heartache?" Or describe someone as a "pain in the butt?" Well, now you are talking about your *enteric nervous system*. Recent discoveries have led researchers to discover that over 100 million neurons exist in the lining of our digestive systems. Scientists have shown that this nervous system not only tells our brain specific things about digestion, such as when we are full about three-quarters into a meal, but that it can actually act independently of brain central.

One of the more interesting findings about our enteric nervous system is its ability to help us get out of the doldrums by ordering up some of mom's home cooking. Say you've had a really tough day and are feeling kind of down. You feel like you need something that is going to help you to just feel like you are getting a hug from mom. You are not sure exactly what you want, but you keep thinking meatloaf and potatoes or macaroni and cheese. It seems as if the nerves in your gut are signaling the brain to order up some good old comfort food that will help you see that all can be well with the world. Before you know it, your limbic system is feeling a bit better and releasing positive hormones.

Get Your Mind Straight

In today's world, people are constantly complaining about the volume of information that we're drowning in via the Internet and its search engines, social media, and daily e-mail blasts from well-intentioned thought leaders. That doesn't even begin to count the endless reams of information we try to process at work from spreadsheets to dashboard reports. The truth is that we are overloaded with data. I often hear that we have plenty of data but not much information. We're oftentimes not able to take the time to process what we know and instead just react to what we read or see. Without an ability to gain some perspective on all the information we take in, it seems impossible to react to situations in any way but a full-fledged stressed-out response.

It's not just individuals who want to understand more about how we can effectively manage all the information we have to process, but also leading organizations. Companies such as General Mills, Google, Shell Oil, and GlaxoSmithKline, among scores of others, have begun offering classes and training programs to help their employees become more skilled in dealing with stressful situations in real time. Their approach is to share the practice of mindfulness.

I'm always careful when I talk with corporate leaders about mindfulness as it is sometimes viewed as being a little "woo-woo." Since meditation and mindfulness is not native to our Western culture, many people look at it as some far-out Eastern thing. Of course, nothing could be further from the truth, but we do have to deal in a world where biases and prejudices operate. Interestingly, as I've traveled around the country speaking to companies about resilience, I am beginning to hear questions from leaders about mindfulness training. Much like how it took 20 years to address tobacco use and obesity in our lives, we may now be on the brink of transformational thinking about new ways to use our minds.

Mindfulness provides an easy approach for us to understand a simple strategy for improving how we think about our day. Mindfulness can be defined as *the intentional act of paying attention to the events around us in a non-judgmental and open manner*. It is actually something most of us do every day, but not intentionally. It is, however, something that we *can* be intentional about and find ways to build into our day to help us be more resilient to stress in real time.

My favorite example of how we are mindful is innocently watching children at play. I have a little granddaughter, Kyra, who is four years old. When she is swinging gleefully at the playground or creating an entire family event with her dolls, she is a sheer joy to watch. I watch her with a sense of love and pleasure that just allows me to enjoy the moment. Mindfulness creates a kind of perspective that leaves us watching and appreciating our own and others' points of views in a non-critical manner.

Developed by Jon Cabot-Zinn in the 1970s while he was at the Massachusetts Medical School, mindfulness builds on meditative practices, but can be done at any time of the day and in any situation. The technique is relatively simple to learn and the opportunities to use it only require that you are mindful enough to remember to try it out. Here are a few simple tools to try, whether at work, at home, or in between:

- **Pay attention to your breathing**. Many of us have done this exercise in our stress management classes, but have you done it in your regular day? Take a look at a batter in a baseball game as he faces a critical pitch. He almost always takes a deep breath to collect his thoughts. He is focusing his mind on the flight of the ball coming his way.
- **Notice what is going on around you**. This is similar to my example about watching granddaughter Kyra. You can try this out at your next staff meeting. Pay attention to who seems really relaxed and who is a bit tighter. What happens when the boss walks in, and what work gets done during the meeting? Even pay attention to how you act during the session and whether your contributions are creating value.
- **Let your urges pass**. A mindfulness teacher once pointed out to me that if I get a feeling or idea coming through my head, it was not necessary to overly focus, ruminate, or even do anything about it. Remember our exercise earlier about e-mail? Next time you have that urge, just let it pass. Your messages will be there in an hour.
- **Pay attention to your body's physical sensations**. We discussed our various nervous systems, all of which provide important information about our world. See what happens if you listen to that gut instinct and act on it.

Here are some simple exercises to begin developing a mindfulness mindset in your life at work and at home:

- **The walking mind.** We all take walks during our day and perhaps one of yours takes you outside. When you do, instead of thinking about the tasks you have to get done when you get home tonight, try paying attention to your walk. Notice the people around you, the pace and speed of your steps. Try walking in rhythm with your breathing and see if you can create a little cadence between the two. Try slowing down for some of the walk and speed up for some of it.

- **The foodie mind.** How often do you notice, really notice, what you are eating? Some people are mindful when it comes to drinking a glass of wine. When the sommelier at the restaurant brings over a wine to sample, we may swirl it in our mouth checking for its fragrance and bouquet. It may take years of practice to develop a palette sophisticated enough to distinguish the subtleties of a great wine, but when we practice doing so, we are using mindfulness tools. What if we tried that same exercise with a fruit that is in the lineage of wine? Head over to your pantry and pull out a box of raisins and pick a solitary raisin to get to know it a little better. Focus on what it feels like in your hand, place it to your nose, and draw on its aroma. Place it in your mouth and notice its texture before biting into it and allowing the explosion of that singular flavor to burst onto your tongue.

- **Mindful ears.** Pick out a song from your music library or one you've never heard before from the Spotify app. Put on your headphones, so you can really hear the sounds and words of the artist. Don't judge the music or criticize the lyrics, but instead just listen in and imagine the singer in her studio. Imagine that you might be sitting right next to her taking in all the sights and sounds.

- **Mindful you.** Every day we engage in mindless routines that are automated within our routine. Brushing our teeth, checking e-mail when we get into work, taking a mid-afternoon break for a Starbucks latté, heading to the gym after work. These routines are great in that we have them built into our daily activities. Building in some mindfulness may mean changing some of these patterns, so you gain a new perspective on how you run each day. Try using your non-dominant hand to brush your teeth. Forget about the latté at Starbucks and try a new iced tea combination. Reverse your workout, so you do cardio last and really emphasize a different aspect of your strength work. Shifting routines shifts thinking.

- **Mindful stillness.** When he went to Google to do a presentation on his book, *Success Through Stillness: Meditation Made Simple,* music entrepreneur and hip hop artist Russell Simmons talked about the idea that if we can take the simplicity of quietness that we enjoy during a sunset and build it into our everyday life through the practice of meditation, we can improve our daily awareness of how we interact with the world and promote a sense of well-being and happiness for ourselves and others.[xlvii]
- Building a mindfulness mindset merely requires a sense of self-awareness and a few minutes of practice. There are no expectations of you being anyone's guru except your own.

Grace Under Pressure

Being able to handle stress in real time not only means that we are mindful about our actions, but also that we are flexible. Despite our discussion about planning as a way of getting ahead of our stressful situations, we often find that even our best laid plans do not come to fruition. Life can seem to be improvisational much of the time where we have to find alternative solutions to difficult situations through our cleverness and awareness of what might just work in any one situation. Imagine this situation and ask how you would handle it.

I attended a meeting where one of my clients was conducting a major keynote presentation on an initiative he had been working on for over 6 months. He started off great with a few jokes and a hand-raising survey with the audience, all of which connected him with his audience. As he started to work through his PowerPoint presentation, he got a thumb up from his boss. He felt like he had his audience right where he wanted them.

Suddenly, the bulb in the projector blew out and his screen went black, just as he was about to talk about the key aspects of the program. He made a little joke about paying his Staples bill and looked around the room for the audiovisual person who was helping him out, but soon realized no one was around and he was on his own. What do you think he did? What would you have done? Consider your options for a moment, while we share a few stories of grace under pressure.

The 1999 US Women's Soccer team grew up together. Several members began playing together as high school sophomores, then matured into a sports icon that inspired the next group of women players who won the 2015 World title. This group had few role models to follow, so they paved their own path. As they weaved their way through that world championship tournament held in the United States, they gained strength from one another and their belief in what they could do.

In their final game against China, the score was tied and the game moved into penalty kicks. The US women were loose as they began the overtime, almost as if it was just another practice session. After a few successful kicks, the team still needed one insurance goal to secure the victory. Brandi Chastain, one of the team's leaders, proceeded to confidently kick the winning goal in the top right corner of the net. Asked what she was thinking later on, she said, "It's one of the moments you train for and you learn through team building how to live in that moment and everything's going to be okay no matter what you do … just not allowing that moment to be bigger than a 12 yard kick."[xlviii] Grace under pressure.

When Seventh Generation CEO Jeff Hollander returned from a business trip in 2007 to his corporate offices in Burlington VT, he realized that he had no idea what his teams were working on in their offices. Writing in a *Harvard Business Review* article, Hollander, who founded and built the company in 1989, began with a vision to provide green household cleaning and personal care products that nurtured the environment. He had grown the company from $100,000 that first year to over $93 million in revenues and had a target goal of $250 million. He knew his mission was more than just growing revenues, but doing so in a responsible manner.

He described how he challenged himself with issues of urgency, transparency and ensuring that the corporate mission was maintained. He realized and acknowledged that his own weaknesses and lack of interest in business matters such as logistics and IT had cost the company growth opportunities. He decided that he needed to make a change and proceeded to write a business plan to present to his board for a leadership transition. They were stunned that he would take such action, he reported, but by the time the process was completed, and the board had brought in a more experienced CEO who could lead the company toward

their next phase of growth, he knew that he had done the right thing.[xlix]
Grace under pressure.

When I attended my first performance of the Broadway show, *The Book of Mormon*, I wondered what the Mormon Church thought about the play. After all, the same people who produced the irreverent *South Park* cartoon series wrote the play and it is filled with mocking humor and raunchy musical numbers. As I was drifting through my *Playbill*, there, right in the middle of the program was an ad sponsored by the Church, "You've seen the play, now read the Book."

Although the official position of the Mormon Church was to accept the play on its own merits, they certainly did not do what many others expected of them, which was to broadly protest its production. Instead, they went with the flow, used it to their advantage, and took a challenging and potentially difficult situation and turned it into a positive. Grace under pressure.

Getting back to my client with the PowerPoint and blown projector bulb, how did he handle the situation? After looking around the room and finding no help, he pulled up his stool and started telling the story about his initiative. He told his colleagues about his visits to customers and what he was hearing. He shared about the sales calls he made, and what he had heard and learned from people within the company.

He shared his view of the competitive landscape and why he thought a change was necessary. *His PowerPoint was convincing but his story was persuasive.* He knew his details solidly enough that he could easily transition to the story more than the facts. He won them over by being in the moment and successfully navigating his stress. Grace under pressure.

How can you develop your grace under pressure? Here are some ways to find your poise:

- **Create "what if" scenarios.** No telling what might happen during some big event. Write down best case and worst case and think about how you'll handle whatever comes up.
- **Keep things simple.** We tend to overcomplicate our lives thinking that more data is better, but it is difficult to store lots of information in our head and then bring it up in a cogent way. I like the rule of three. Bring out three key ideas that you

think are essential and people will view you as being smooth as silk.

- **Own the reality**. We have a tendency to try to explain things away or to remove blame from where it firmly belongs. Yet the old adage of "honesty is the best policy," may be the best way to stay calm when everything else is whirling around.
- **Spread the joy**. Anxiety is contagious and you do not want to spread it or catch it. If others are talking about how bad a situation is or how nervous they are about a project not going well, look to what is working and present that perspective. Sure, you want to acknowledge the downside but if you are going to do that, it is only fair to recognize the upside.

Travis Graham graduated as class valedictorian from the University of Tennessee Law School in 1998. At his commencement address, he told his assembled colleagues that his comments would only take two minutes of their time. He told them he went back through his mind thinking about his law school days, but not find anything revealing enough that could summarize his thoughts about what they would need to take out into the world to become successful. Sitting at his dining room table just a few days before commencement, he came upon a prepared package of breakfast biscuits. As he surveyed the package right there in front of him, he saw the inspiration he knew was the correct message to share with his colleagues. Its simplicity was powerful and true. "Keep cool. But do not freeze."

CHAPTER 6

Bouncing Back and Ahead

In this last section about the Resilience Continuum, we'll discuss the importance of understanding the full impact of a stress situation and why responding quickly and efficiently is important in ensuring a positive outcome to even the most negative events.

Stress is cumulative. It adds up over the course of a day, a week, and a year. You know it. When you've had a particularly difficult day, you feel exhausted and sometimes you just need to go home, put your feet up, and take some time to rest.

Rest is a key aspect of recovery, but for many of us, we want to get back in the game as soon as possible. It is important to recharge our batteries, but the excitement of life is just around the corner and awaits us as soon as we start to regain our energy.

Recovery is so much more than just returning to our normal state of being. How we respond to events after they occur is what successful bounce back is all about. In some situations, it may mean returning to our previous state of balance. In other situations, it may be just working to gain as much as we can in a no-win arrangement. In still others, it may be about looking for an opportunity to grow, even when we are facing what looks like a lost cause. In this chapter, we'll share some stories of how quick action created highly favorable outcomes in business and personal careers. Furthermore, we'll look at how we can take action to change situations where we may have felt powerless, so that even the most difficult events can yield results that change our own and other's perspectives.

A Fire in the Factory

Yossi Sheffi, MIT engineering professor, in his book, *The Resilient Enterprise*, tells the story about a seemingly small and innocuous fire that started on

March 17, 2000. It was the result of a thunderstorm strike to a high-voltage line that fed electricity to a Philips Electronics cell phone chip-manufacturing plant in Albuquerque, NM. The plant staff responded quickly to the fire and by the time fire fighters arrived at the scene, the fire was extinguished.

What made the results of the fire difficult was that it occurred in a "clean room," required to be one of the purest work environments in the world—kept 10,000 times cleaner than a hospital operating room. Although the smoke and water damage was significant, the Phillips team believed they could complete the cleanup job in a week.

As a matter of policy, they alerted their two largest customers, Nokia and Ericsson, who were arch cell phone rivals, to alert them to the event. Phillips accounted for about 40 percent of the chip manufacturing for both companies and they assured them both that the facility would be back to full production without a glitch to their delivery schedule. Phillips estimated it would take a week to return the facility to 100 percent production.

Responses to crises are different among people and organizations, and success often lies in our ability to recognize the importance of an appropriate response. That happens for us personally, as well as for organizations.

When Nokia received word of the fire, their response strategy for addressing the crisis was to bump it up on their priority management list. They knew there could be issues for Phillips in recovering from the fire, and they monitored and tracked the facility's progress on a daily rather than on a weekly basis. Their protocols had shifted over the previous several years when they found that their production partners might sometime report a rosier prediction on problems than actually exists.

Over at Ericsson, experience told them that Phillips was a trusting and believable partner and that they did not need to take any independent action.

Tracking progress on a daily basis meant that within 7 to 10 days, Nokia knew that the repairs would likely take more than the one week Phillips promised. In considering the consequences of the situation, Nokia recognized that their productions would be severely impacted. They immediately took action to address the potential problems that included (1) modifying the chip design so chips could be made at other Phillips facilities, (2) pressing Phillips to shift production to other plants, and (3) looking for alternative vendors for production. All three actions were addressed rapidly and they had all options for alternative production identified and in place within a few days.

Ericsson's more trusting approach and their schedule of information input led them to not discover the enormity of the problems until almost three weeks after the fire—when it was much too late to do too much about it. Their archrival Nokia had already locked up alternative production facilities and had found other producers who could supply them with the chips they needed.

Ericsson's cell phone production was stymied. When the company filed its quarterly report in July of that year, they reported that the fire had caused a $200 million operating loss and that earnings would be below expectation for the full year. At the close of the fiscal year, Ericsson told its shareholders that it had lost $1.68 billion in its cell phone division and 3 percent of its market share. Their woes continued as their market share shrank, forcing them to merge their cell phone division with Sony. Ericsson never bounced back, whereas Nokia responded more effectively and used the experience to grow market share and revenues.[1]

Disruptions happen all the time. Companies experience them as corporate crises, sometime small, sometimes big. For individuals, we experience them as stressful events. In both cases, *our ability to respond effectively determines whether we bounce back effectively or not.*

Connecting business resilience and personal resilience is important. Your company's supply chain experts are highly aware of the dangers that can occur from situations, such as the fire at the Phillips plant. They line up multiple suppliers and maintain strong relationships with vendors to ensure a steady flow of materials, so that your company can continue to produce products.

Bounce back opportunities come our way all the time, as we have to deal with stressful situations. Like the story of Phillips, Nokia, and Ericsson, individual bounce-back stories tell how we can use different strategies to help us recover from all kinds of business challenges.

As we've discussed previously, we know that bounce back is central to our traditional view of resilience, and that recovery from difficulties is hardwired into our DNA. Achieving recovery, however, is only part of the equation. *More important is the quality of the recovery.* Is our bounce back minimally effective in terms of not being impeded by the negative event

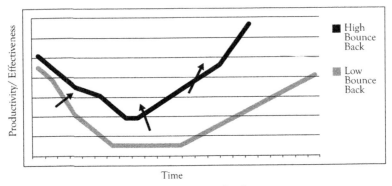

Figure 6.1 Stressful Event and Bounce back

or do we use that event to grow and gain a better perspective and new skills that will help us do better in the future?

In the graph shown in Figure 6.1, you will see that in both situations, people will generally recover from a negative situation. This graph shows what happens to our productivity over time when we face a stressful event. What we typically see is that our productivity and effectiveness are diminished. Remember, we have little choice over how our bodies respond initially to stress, so seeing a dip in performance is not surprising. As we begin our recovery process, our effectiveness returns. In the scenario where we have high bounce back, the recovery phase begins faster and moves to a higher level of performance, even exceeding our previous state. In the low bounce back situation, we are slower to recover and our bounce back merely returns to our pre-stress level.

There are a number of factors that contribute to becoming a high bounce back person who exceeds the prior state.

The first factor is how quickly we recover from the adverse event. Speed of response is important in bounce back. We don't want to linger in a negative place any longer than necessary, so finding a path to recovery as quickly as possible is important. However, we also want to make certain that we take sufficient time to figure out the essential steps toward our end goal.

The second factor is using energy efficiently. Stress is a tremendous utilizer of energy. Not only do we have to deal with the physiological drain on our system, but the mental toll that stress takes on us violently pulls us away from clear thinking and sound decision making. Being efficient in how we return to our level of functioning helps the recovery and allows us to return or exceed our previous state in a more resource-wise manner.

Leap While the Iron Is Hot

A few years ago, I had the opportunity to coach a fellow named John, who was a senior leader in a New York–based financial institution. During the financial crisis of 2008, his company had asset difficulties and was acquired by another institution. Everyone at his company was shocked and scrambling to figure out what the acquisition meant to the institution and to them. Some of the acquired people were fearful that this turn of events would change the culture of their company and ex-pressed anger and disdain for the new company. Although John was not panicked about the acquisition, he was concerned about what this change would mean for his customers, his colleagues, and himself.

When John was invited to his new boss's office to meet him and his new coworkers, they met in a large conference room. When they sat down, John immediately saw his worst fears coming to life. There were literally (and figuratively) not enough seats at the table for everyone and he and several other staff members had to go into another room to bring in a chair for themselves. John's new manager chuckled about that situation and while everyone had a good laugh, the reality of the circumstances was not lost on anyone.

While John was returning home from his meeting, he called me to discuss the situation. With a bit of panic in his voice, he began asking questions: "How should I deal with my new boss? Can I recover my previous role or will I be demoted? Is there an opening anywhere in the business group that will allow me to see a career path? Should I start looking for another position with another company?"

We decided to meet in person the next day. Although everyone around him was sure things would go from bad to worse, we used our coaching sessions to explore all of John's options. I suggested that perhaps there was a great opportunity hidden in what looked like a major crisis. Instead of just thinking about how he could hold onto his job, what if he decided that he would be bold and go after higher-level roles with more responsibility. It's the idea that is hidden in the Chinese characters for crisis, 危机, which is metaphorically depicted to mean *dangerous opportunity*. Is it possible to look at a situation that appears at face value to be perilous and see within it a chance for greatness?

John soon recognized that he didn't have to just sit back and wait for something to happen. Whether or not his boss had a plan for him was irrelevant, it was time for him to make a plan for himself.

When he returned to his office, John ignored all the negativity around him and called his new boss. He told him he was excited about the merger and saw all kinds of possibilities for efficiencies and opportunities for growth. He told him he was going to work on a plan that he would have ready in one month that would spell out the capabilities of his team and how their efforts could dovetail with the priorities of the company. He would reach out to his new colleagues during that period, getting to know them and their teams better, and using that time to get a feel and understanding for his new company's culture. While everyone else around him was complaining about their new company, John was embracing it. Finally, John told his boss that if there were any projects, issues, and problems that he could be of assistance in addressing, he was ready to step up to the plate and take a swing. His boss told him he appreciated his enthusiasm and would look forward to seeing his plan.

Over the next month, John did a good job of developing his plan. He made several trips to meet new colleagues, took the opportunity to interview his own team to gain their perspective on their roles, and participated in industry benchmarking with consultants. All this led him to write a first-class plan that he shared with his new boss.

After reviewing the plan, his manager told him that he appreciated the plan but that he would have to do another one, because the company had decided to offer him an expanded role within the group. They decided to split roles, and John was going to add new responsibilities onto his current role. Fifty new people joined his group as a consolidation and reassignments were made. He was thrilled by the opportunity and challenge and took it in with increased excitement. He had made the leap, successfully addressing the challenge of his company's merger and had even exceeded his previous role. He had gone beyond bouncing back.

He leaped forward.

Consider three key factors that we saw play out in our two examples above: (1) focusing on returning, at least, to the previous state of functioning and, ideally, exceeding it; (2) doing so in a rapid fashion by learning quickly and responding effectively; and (3) being efficient in not wasting time in doing things that are not productive and could create a set-back situation.

The challenge of our dealing with stressful situations is that we often don't think we know how they are going to turn out. We are often taken aback by our biological response. Our negativity bias creates the potential of our worse case thinking. It freezes us into inaction instead of looking for the possibilities of a "best case" outcome.

Our negative thinking and loss aversion tendency (which is our fear of not wanting to lose anything, such as an investment in a stock or hoping that our clients renew their contract for at least as much as they spent last year) means that if we can just get back to our previous state of functioning, then we'll be doing just fine.

For both Nokia and John, the recognition of potential opportunity that existed within the crises they were facing was not initially perceived. For Nokia, it was merely a plan to ensure that they could continue to run their production facilities at the same pace that they had been doing previously. It wasn't until they rearranged their chip formulation to ensure that they had vendors who could produce chips that they, perhaps, came to realize that they had an opportunity to take market share from Ericsson and grow their business.

John was initially just looking to hold onto his job. Seeing that there were not enough seats around the table meant that he had to take some kind of action to merely return to his current state of action. John went beyond that effort by recognizing that he had value that he could bring to his new employer. By focusing on doing his job (building his plan) and by offering to take on any and all new tasks, he demonstrated that he was actually ready to do more than take a seat at the table. He could move closer to the head of it.

The effort to improve the situation rather than merely settle for a return to past conditions is depicted in Figure 6.2. Instead of "fixing" and returning to the past, John innovated and created an even better future.

Speed is the second important quality. Nokia had a process in place for ensuring that timeliness related to reviews of critical situations was

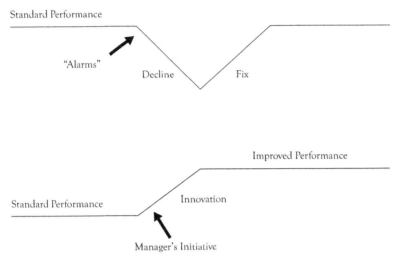

Figure 6.2 Restoration vs. Innovation

in place. For Nokia, however, it was more than that. They had created a culture where individuals effectively communicated with one another and were able to express the sense of urgency that was required to address the issue. The Nokia team, recognizing that time was of the essence, came together quickly to put together alternative options. Ericsson failed to have a Plan B.

John recognized the old adage, "You have only one chance to make a first impression," and maximized his opportunities. While his peers and colleagues were expressing their fear and concern about what the merger would mean for them professionally and personally, John was already on his game, offering to address the critical issues that he could see the firm would need to successfully move forward. By reaching out quickly to his boss, he not only showed that he was ready to respond to the challenges facing the firm but that he could be counted on to step up to the plate.

Finally, being efficient is effective. We do not want to use any more energy than necessary when we are in high stress situations. When my daughter was young, she would go off to sleep on her own. She didn't need prodding from her parents to go to bed. She would rub her eyes and say, "I'm tired," and would head off to sleep. She didn't waste extra energy fighting her fatigue, so she could watch an extra half hour of TV. She was efficient in recognizing that she needed to recharge her batteries and got to the work at hand (which was sleeping).

In a similar manner, both examples above were efficient in how they approached recovering from their work challenges. Nokia immediately recognized that there could be a potential problem and mobilized the right people to make decisions and take actions. They didn't agonize over what to do, nor did they make the scene overly dramatic. There was no screaming at Phillips for the fire or their possible misrepresentation of time frames. Instead, they decided what needed to be done and took the appropriate action with little fanfare.

John, on the other hand, was driven a bit by fear of what could happen. However, once he recognized what he needed to do, he moved through his options and steps with relative ease. This is one of the great advantages of having an efficiency approach to addressing stressful situations. Once you make up your mind and set a course, don't question yourself. Move through your plan and minimize additional work and effort for yourself. If your plan is flawed, you'll have a chance to modify it as you go along. John had to make numerous changes to his business case while he was drafting it, but it did not take away from the core effort of building a plan that he could present to his new boss.

Building Our Response-Ability

In 16th-century Europe, people believed that swans could only be white. That was the normal expectation. That was the case until Dutch explorer William de Viamingh traveled to Western Australia and discovered black swans. His old-world colleagues were astounded by the fact that an entire new breed of swans existed. For them, it was a highly unexpected event.

Author Nicholas Taleb, in his 2007 book *The Black Swan*, describes a modern day interpretation of the term by talking about how people and organizations respond to highly stressful but highly unpredictable events.[li] Examples of black swan events include the terrorist attacks of 9/11, or the stock market crash of 1929. These events, which are rare in their occurrence, bring high stress to the culture. It is even possible to have positive black swan events, such as when we hear of a single mother factory worker winning a $300 million lottery—something that brings a smile to our faces.

An oversimplification of Taleb's thesis is to say that since we cannot predict these kinds of events, in order to successfully grow from them, we must build robustness into our systems, working to mitigate the downside of a possible event while exploiting the upside of possible good events.

I remember my son-in-law, a banker, calling me in October of 2008 suggesting that I make sure that I have several thousand dollars of cash on hand. He was not so sure that the banking system, which was under significant stress during those early days of the financial crisis, wouldn't collapse and leave everyone with limited access to cash. Thankfully it did not happen here but we saw in 2015 where that very occurrence happened in Greece.

Although most personal difficulties in our lives are rarely black swans, some of us may describe them as "gray swans." They are not disruptive enough to throw our lives into total chaos as might happen with the death of a spouse or the sudden and unexpected loss of a job, but challenging enough to cause the disturbing stress reactions that set our lives a bit asunder.

In a subsequent book, *Antifragile: Things That Gain From Disorder*, Taleb continues his discussion on how we respond to stressful events by coining the term "antifragile." To Taleb, fragile systems, whether they are corporate, cultural, or individual, break down in the face of stressful events and merely seek a return to a calm and tranquil existence.[lii] They may struggle just trying to maintain their balance with a strategy of protecting to the downside to make sure things don't get any worse—a bit like our thinking about how the "stress management" model just tries to keep us focused on maintaining a status quo.

I see fragility in the faces of many employees who just hope they can hold onto their jobs under today's tough economic conditions instead of thinking about how they can find ways to bring value to their organizations that will help advance the mission and their own success.

The antifragile individual, however, looks for challenges and even chaos to grow beyond what their original state of existence could be. In what is sometimes described as *posttraumatic growth*, the antifragile individual sees the opportunity in their stressful situation and their strategy goes beyond mere recovery to growth.

This can happen only if we recognize as individuals that we have the capability and responsibility to look at any situation and explore the opportunity for growth that exists within.

My wife, Sheila, has an expression she uses when she is facing what she calls "tough stuff." In her book, *Warrior Mother*, she tells the story of how our family dealt with the death of two of our children, our son, Ken, from AIDS in 1997 and our daughter, Corinne, from breast cancer in 2004.[liii] Upon hearing of Corinne's diagnosis, Sheila began using her daily showers as "venting chambers," where that tiny protective stall allowed for soundproofing for her grief and rage. As a lifelong professional dancer, social worker, improvisational artist, and author, Sheila would sing her grief by repeating her own made-up song based on the foundation of the words, "What good can come from this?" For weeks she continued to cry out her grief, hoping that it would somehow move or transform her pain into something better.

Sheila and I are part of an international improvisational art community known as Interplay. We use all forms of improv including singing, dancing, and storytelling to explore varied life issues. Unlike most improv with which people are familiar, Interplay is not just comedy-focused. This improv is about real life and explores everything within the full range of the human experience. We've traveled the world performing Interplay's foremost performance program called "The Unbelievable Beauty of Being Human."

It was during the time of Corinne's illness that we traveled with a group of Interplayers to Australia to perform at the University of Sydney. Corinne insisted that we go, as she knew how important art was to her mother and that in order to sustain caregiving, Sheila needed to recharge her batteries. Interplay provided that refueling.

During the last night of the performance run, the typical juicy stuff had been explored, such as babies, love, food, and flowers. On the list that had been drawn from the audience was also cancer, and when our group leader, Cynthia, called on Sheila to perform, she was ready to go. Performing along with several other Interplayers who would dance to her singing, Sheila began, as she had done for months already, with her slow lamentation of "What good can come from this?"

In her book, *Warrior Mother*, she describes how the performance began to move her words and energy,

> What GOOD, what GOOD, what GOOD can come from THIS?
>
> And then the song began to change. In the Greek tradition of stage as alter and dance and theater as healing arts, a softening came into my voice, into my whole body. The song became a prayer: "GOOD can come from this." The prayer turned into a pledge and promise, "GOOD WILL COME FROM THIS. GOOD WILL COME FROM THIS." In the aftermath, as the song resonated throughout my body, I began to feel, for the first time, that it would.[liv]

No one would fault a mother for being fragile in the face of losing two children. Sheila has found her way to create good from the tragedy through the time she provided to our children as caregiver, and then continued with her relationship with her grandchildren, in her writings about how people can deal with what she calls "tough stuff," and in using her art to help others heal from their personal tragedies.

Being able to respond to these kinds of challenges is about not giving up and even recognizing our own responsibility to address them. We can heighten our response-ability by using several strategies to grow through adversity:

- **Focus on small gains while keeping your larger goals in play.** Recovering and growing in the bounce-back phase can create a great deal of turbulence. You will be bothered by the memories or impact of the stressful event and you'll be seeking ways to recover and grow from it. Incremental improvement is essential and giving yourself a time frame to work on these gains is very helpful.
- **Simplify life.** Energy drain is a killer when you are in recovery mode, so you want to simplify things as much as you can. Building in routines that automate your life can help

you achieve some success. Set your schedule at work so it has a regular pattern, such as checking e-mail at specific times during day instead of constantly. Make sure you have agendas for all meetings. Get TSA Pre-Check, so that you can ease your way through security at the airport.

- **Hang around with people who are on your side.** It is too easy for others to give advice, hoping that somehow their ideas will help you. Make sure these folks have "skin in the game," in that they've had similar experiences or are committed to your growth. Too many people want to give unsolicited advice, but you don't have to listen.

- **Have a mantra**. A mantra is a statement or idea that you repeat mentally as a way of both relaxing yourself and focusing your intentions. The Serenity Prayer represents a mantra for those seeking peace of mind. Steve Jobs would use the mantra "focus and simplicity," as a way of helping direct the workings of Apple. For Sheila, it was "Good can come from this."

- **Rest is part of the journey**. We hear a lot about not getting enough sleep and most of us know the importance of rest. No doubt many of us disregard this information and do so at a price that may result in bad moods, decreased work performance, and feeling tired. I prefer not to make people feel bad about not getting enough rest and instead point out that the degree of rest each of us requires is very individualized. If you are able to take a quick nap on the bus ride home, that is great. If you need a solid seven hours of sleep, go for it. Vegging out on the sofa is restorative so enjoy your downtime

- **Have a Plan B.** Taleb talks about nature's tendency to build redundancy into its systems. We have two lungs and two kidneys, just in case one fails. Having a recovery plan that provides backup systems means that we have choices on how we deal with situations that may go further awry. When returning from vacation, I like to schedule my return for a Saturday or noon on Sunday, so in case my flight is delayed or

canceled, I can still make it back with time to unpack my bags
and get ready for Monday's workday.

- **Have a community of friends.** Sheila found great support
  and reliance from others in her Interplay and work
  communities. People soon got past the awkwardness of being
  afraid of "asking the wrong question," about the status of
  our daughter's health and instead focused on the important
  question of "How can we help?"

We can't keep bad things from happening to us and we can't keep good
things from happening to us. Having our plan to recover *and* grow
from those events, we make resilience such a powerful force for good
in our lives.

PART 3

Putting It into Action

Inertia is a powerful force. Newton's first law of physics tells us that an object at rest tends to stay at rest and an object in motion tends to stay in motion. As psychologists we know that Newton's Laws don't just apply to objects in outer space, but also to people and their inner space. Although making changes may never be easy, we may also have a tendency to make them harder on ourselves than is necessary. In this section, we'll examine strategies for change and identify the kinds of small but significant steps each of us can take to begin to turn the tables on stress. This allows us to stop being victims to stress and instead become victors over stress.

In Chapter 7, we examine why being negative is hardwired into our existence and why it is important to have that approach. Yet, we want to recognize that we do not want to live there but just visit. In much the same way, positivity is equally hard-wired into us and we present ways to rewire our brains for the upside.

Chapter 8 is all about the ways you can invest your time and energy to become a happier and more resilient person. We discuss the importance of our mindset in seeing the world differently and provide seven tools to help you find more delight in your life. Our formula for building your Rresilience IQ takes in all the factors related to how we approach our stress at work and at home, and gives us a formula method for maximizing our resilience return.

Finally, in Chapter 9, we share ideas for both you and your workplace leaders about how to bring a daily dose of success to your job and career. We debunk the ideas about our having two separate lives (a work life and a home life), and explain how we actually have just one life. We introduce the latest research-based ideas about how to increase effectiveness and pleasure at work, and provide an entire section for leaders about their role in building resilience in the workplace.

CHAPTER 7

Overcoming Your Negativity Bias: Creating Your Future and Not Accepting Your Lot

We are biologically programmed to think negatively. And it is a good thing. Managing potential dangers is a far more important survival strategy than being a Pollyanna and hoping that everything will somehow just work out.

Research on risk and reward tells us that the pain of loss (financial, for example) inflicts much more pain than the amount of pleasure we feel from the successes in our lives, so it makes sense that we protect ourselves against danger and loss. That is important to remember as we build our resilience and recognize that thinking negatively is not a sign of weakness but is instead an indication that we are making ourselves sure we are safe.

What if, however, we were able to rewire our brain, so that the preponderance of negative thinking doesn't take such a prominent role in our day-to-day activities? We'll examine ways that can change our brain thinking, so that we build hardiness against negativity and create new ways to create the future we want.

The Seduction of Negative Thinking

Let's establish that "it's good to think bad."

It can be a dangerous world out there. Maslow's foundation in his famous hierarchy is for survival[lv] (Figure 7.1). Every college freshman encounters this (or at least they once did when there were liberal arts curricula):

If we're threatened at the physiological level, we're encountering "bad stuff" around us.

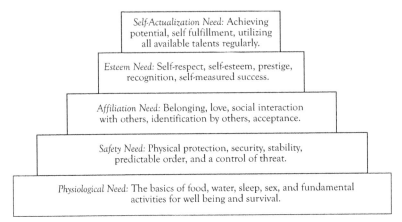

Figure 7.1 Maslow's Hierarchy of Needs

The correct degree of vigilance is important for our protection. Whether it was walking on the Serengeti during primitive times, when predators were common and protection crude, or driving defensively on today's interstate highways, we need to be aware of *potential* danger, not solely the danger we see. By "correct degree," I mean stopping short of the paranoid. The screeners at the security points in airports today are relieved frequently, because you cannot remain at a high degree of vigilance in otherwise boring and mundane jobs (staring at monitors or, for that matter, staffing ICBM silos).

Nonetheless, there is a value in negative thinking, and we should escape from the rubrics of "stop being so negative" when, in fact, it is only prudent to do so. For example, if you overpromise something to a customer, you're sunk. Even if you deliver well, it's not going to be enough.

"This will be the most successful promotion of all time."

"We're going to break sales records."

"This will be the party to end all parties."

No matter how good, it's not what was promised.

But when you under-promise and over-deliver, you've changed the mindset. To do this, you need to be able to think of "worst case." What happens if I promise the moon but only deliver Chicago? There is wisdom

Marshall McLuhan: "The price of eternal vigilance is indifference."

in creating dynamics where you try to ensure success *but also protect your-self from venturing into unavoidable failure.*

In some companies—and in some relationships—no matter how successful you are, you just can't "win enough."

Great year, Trudy, but of course not quite as good as you did last year.

The most important lesson is that while some negative thinking is inescapable and probably quite prudent, we can become victims of the sirens' song of negativity and adopt it as a lifestyle and business strategy. And that's what we are warning you to stay away from, loud and clear.

We tend to give *more credibility* to negative ideas than to positive ones. Research has shown that our brains react more powerfully to negative possibilities (fear about survival) than positive possibilities (hope in some potential). The more immediate gratification tends to be protection, not innovation, certainty and not risk.

A research study by Tiffany Ito and her colleagues at Ohio State University showed that students, when shown positive images (e.g., a Ferrari or tempting food) or negative images (e.g., a dead cat or a lost cause) produced different brain activity responses. Neutral pictures, such as a hair dryer or fire hydrant, produced disinterested responses. She discovered that the negative response generated a greater surge in electrical activity than positive or neutral images. She concluded that our emotions *are most influenced by negative events and that biologically we are still programmed to focus more on the negative.*[lvi]

More obvious examples of this can be seen in the media daily. The approaches used in local news programming, for example, are highly negative: threats, floods, accidents, disasters, and disappointments. The "good news" is usually a human interest story about a lost cat reunited with its owners—after some harrowing experience. Listen to the sound bites and read the headlines. You'll never hear "Record number of new jobs created!" but rather "Experts fear record number of new jobs hiding a basic structural flaw in our economy."

Politicians are consistently negative. They all decry the negative ad and mudslinging, but then engage in it with gusto. They are advised daily that negative images arouse more emotion and cause more action than positive ones. They would rather talk about a rumored homophobic statement uttered by the opposition 25 years ago, than talk about their plans to reduce spending and balance the budget in the next four years.

We see rather tasteless comparisons of brand advertising versus "Brand X" and we hear almost hourly of the next food scare: red meat, sugar, salt, gluten, fat, and diet soda. The Internet makes negative rumors far worse and adds to the unscientific noise. If you don't believe that, consider the children dying from measles in the 21st century because their parents are afraid vaccinations will hurt them.

We have to migrate from a default to negative thinking to a natural embrace of positive thinking. We are beyond the survival stage. The Serengeti is no longer a danger, and we are rational enough to know that we should be careful driving, walking down unfamiliar streets, or eating yellow snow.

The Universal Need for Positivity

At the 1968 Summer Olympics in Mexico City, a young Tanzanian athlete named John Stephen Akhwari ran the marathon and finished last. Yet his story perhaps as much as any other runner at that event won the admiration of the world.

Unaccustomed to running at 7,300 feet, Mr. Akhwari suffered leg cramps early in the race but continued to run. At one point, he collided with another runner, fell, badly injured his knee, and dislocated his shoulder, but he continued to run.

The other runners, all world-class athletes, finished the race within the expected range of 2.5 hours, but Akhwari, wounded and in pain, entered the Olympic Stadium a full hour after the second to the last competitor crossed the finish line. Almost all the spectators had left as the award ceremony was over, but soon a vehicle with flashing lights entered the arena to announce that another runner was coming to finish. The few thousand attendees cheered the Tanzanian as he hobbled around the track and crossed the finish line.

In his post-race interview, the media asked why did he even bother to finish the race since he had no chance of winning. Mr. Akhwari was incredulous that such a question was asked and his response shows the capacity of individuals to overcome the negativity bias that pervades our culture and biology. "My country did not send me 5,000 miles to start the race. My country sent me 5,000 miles to finish the race."[lvii]

We have all had experiences that have shown us that we just have to stop being so negative. I tell people all the time that our dogs don't stop at an accidentally open gate and do a needs analysis, or a risk/reward ratio, or assess the upside/downside. They race through an open gate as any self-respecting dog does, consequences to be considered later—usually much later.

Another rainy day on our vacation. (Yes, but we've had four good days out of six so far.) We seem to default to bemoaning our fate rather than putting things in perspective.

The importance of positive thinking (and it's natural companion, positive self-talk) can be seen, empirically, on a daily basis. When we talk about our gratitude, appreciation, hopes, aspirations, prayers, and even wishful thinking, we are guided by the positive. Like our runner above, people don't enter a race or competition merely to finish, they enter to do the very best they can. A "personal best" is often more rewarding than a champion's expected win. I've never heard cheers at a sports event that sounded like this:

"Just try to finish!"

"Go for the bronze!"

"Just don't embarrass yourself!"

This is even truer in business. You don't want to come close to a sale, you want to make the sale. There are no bonuses for "almost" or for merely persevering. (This is why the "rewards for self-esteem" for merely showing up in grade school events are actually so damaging. They don't replicate reality at all and give a false sense of achievement, which will eventually erode self-esteem.) At work, we hope for the best and plan for the worst, and create sometimes elaborate scenarios for both. But we don't sit back and feel that we're doing fine by our mere presence.

Resilient thinking requires that we focus on how to recover from negative, tragic, and traumatic events. Resilience places us back on a positive path after the brief detour of setback.

The following is an excerpt from Alan's soon to be released book, *Million Dollar Maverick:*

> I've found that most people don't trust their own judgment, so they tend to trust *other people's judgment*, which may be entirely wrong for them (or lousy, period). Or they use trial and error, an extremely expensive and risky means to make decisions about their lives.[lviii]

On the left of Figure 7.2 are what we consider the keys to building trust in your own judgment:

1. **Recognition of success**. Know what constitutes success for you. Hint: It should never be perfection, but "merely" the attainment of important goals.
2. **Positive self-talk**. You should start and end the day with the positives in your life, what you intend to accomplish, and what you have accomplished.
3. **Healthy feedback intolerance**. You can't listen to people whom you haven't asked, because unsolicited feedback *is almost always for the sender's benefit*. This conflicts with the "humility school" people who tell you *all* feedback is good feedback. It isn't. Listen only to those you trust and *you ask.*
4. **Appropriate avatars**. Whom do you admire? What traits are important? Everyone talks about Steve Jobs's wonderful stewardship at Apple, but he was an impossible boss, husband, and father.

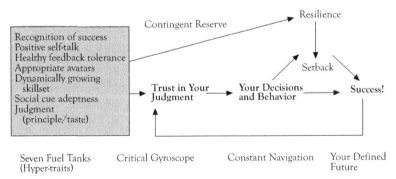

Figure 7.2 Trusting Your Judgment

5. **Dynamically growing skillsets.** Confidence in judgment is buoyed by rising competence in diverse areas.

6. **Social cue adeptness.** You should be able to recognize when to speak and when to listen, which requests are appropriate and inappropriate, when to offer help, and when to mind your own business.

7. **Judgment.** As Jefferson observed, "In matters of taste, swim with the tide; in matters of principle, stand like a rock."[lix]

Your judgment will then lead to better decisions and behavior to achieve your defined future (success), and also serve as a contingent reserve when you experience a setback and need the resilience to bounce back and not be defeated.

I call the seven traits "hyper-traits," and the trust in your own judgment your personal gyroscope, which keeps you on balance, upright, and headed in the right direction.

Think about the most successful—and respected and sought after—people in your business or office. They are universally positive. They provide a ray of light, not a dark dead end. They are people who others want to follow, not avoid. They seem to do more than simply make lemonade when given a lemon, they instead create a lemonade industry.

The cycle is inviolable. Positive people create energy, which others thrive on, which gives them still greater energy because of the highly charged people they've attracted. They are the ones normally chosen to lead, to advise, and to coach.

I tell consultants whom I coach all the time: Enthusiasm in contagious. If you're enthusiastic—positive—your prospects will be, too. When you've met a succession of apathetic customers, the odds are it's not them, it's you. We all give off "vibes," the positive and negative vibes are among the strongest and easiest to detect.

Rewiring our Brains for the Upside

Our brains seem to have an "all or nothing" default. Try this experiment:

Start reading an article at your desk and also turn on some music *that you've not heard before.* Can you read and comprehend the material while listening to the music, especially lyrics? Test your comprehension by writing a summary of the reading *and* of the music. I'm betting you can't do it. The vaunted "multitasking" doesn't always serve as our brain's favorite operating system.

What we consider to be multitasking, in fact, is more accurately "serial-tasking." Our brain moves back and forth, to and fro, *between* activities but we don't *concurrently* focus on activities. (Another example: Have two people speak on each side of you in different conversations, and try to respond to both. This actually happens in many social situations and a lot of bars!)

We really don't focus on two or more activities at the same time, at least not terribly effectively or successfully. We often talk on the phone while trying to pay bills, but the payment or conversation will suffer. This is also why people texting stop dead on the sidewalk, stalling people behind them: They can't text and walk successfully simultaneously! (And this is why texting and driving is so terribly dangerous. Studies have shown that even hands-free phones are dangerous, because people engaged in conversations lose focus on their driving—it's not their hands that are the issue, but their brains.)

Dr. Michael Weisand at the Wright State Research Institute calls the "winner take all" attitude that of the primary brain focus.[ix] For example, if you are perusing a menu at your favor restaurant, and the options include herb-crusted lamb loin, soft-shell crab tempura, sautéed golden rainbow trout, heart of rib eye filet, and cauliflower steak with Indian curry, your mind begins to swirl with the choices. But once you choose, all other options drop off a cliff of contemplation, and you're salivating only for that "winner."

And your mind proceeds to its next task, perhaps the best wine to go with the meal.

Case Study

Union General George McClellan, a renowned martinet, was sometimes found dictating four letters concurrently to four different secretaries when visitors arrived. A subordinate found out later that all four had to be redictated, separately, after the visitors had left.

Most of us deal with stress through negativity bias, as explained previously, so that "winner takes all" is a negative priority when it comes to our perceived stress reduction. We say things such as, "I can't handle stress," or "I'm overwhelmed." We stop thinking about how to overcome—positive interventions—and surrender instead to the notion that we can't overcome the overwhelm. The negative "takes all."

Negative thinking also narrows our thinking. We focus on survival, Maslow's lowest level of need, and limit out choices because we seek only safety and relatively small goals. This can result in unhealthy choices for us: poor diet, easily angered, excessive risk taking. The latter is often manifested by risky driving, excessive gambling, and addictions. We are redirecting self-anger to try to preserve our identity while venting. Our own negative thinking, surrender, and anger limit our thinking about how to *positively* respond to problems.

This is why overcoming negativity bias is so important and such a personal pursuit. Think of the different responses you see every day to relatively minor incidents:

- **A driver cuts you off.**
  Forget about it.
  OR
  Road rage.
- **Someone hits their elbow on a drawer.**
  Laugh and rub it.
  OR
  Curse loudly and scream at whomever opened the drawer.
- **The stock market goes down 200 points.**
  Be happy that you're in it for the long term.
  OR
  Manically call broker and demand changes in portfolio.
- **Your computer freezes.**
  Call for help and move to lap top or other work.
  OR
  Scream at repair people that you want special priority
    response.

- **You're placed on hold by airline.**
  Check your e-mail while you wait.
  OR
  See the and call back repeatedly trying to get someone.

As you can see, these aren't so far-fetched! When you include more major issues, such as a car breakdown on the highway, a warning from the IRS, or a relative taken to the hospital, the response has far more dramatic implications. So the focus we use needs to be positive: What are my options? How can I improve this? What resources are available? This is far better than the negative: Why is God against me? Who invented this crap? Why is my tax money being wasted?

I'm suggesting that positive thinking, in light of the "all or nothing" mentality, requires focus on one task at a time. We have been lulled into thinking that concomitant tasks can be accomplished at once because they seem related. But what the computer seems to do concurrently (which is actually just ferociously fast serial processing) has subverted our thinking about what we are capable of doing well.

We don't order the trout and filet together and eat a bit of both, because they don't complement each other and choosing a wine would be very difficult. We can't expect to write a report and talk on the phone simultaneously and expect both the call and report to be done well let alone listen to music, deal with our small child, pet the dog, figure out how to get the squirrels off the bird feeder outside the window, and worry about the overdrawn amounts in the checkbook!

Yet, that is not only what we tend to do, but we actually have convinced ourselves that we're good at it. We are not. We're terrible at it. And we endanger our decisions at best, and our lives at worst, when we allow that fiction to influence our choices of behavior.

Airline pilots have landed at the wrong airports, have feathered the wrong engine (the cause of a huge Asian air crash not long ago), and used the wrong radio beacon (resulting in a horrible crash in South America). One cockpit recording of a commercial airline crash in California, caused by hitting a smaller plane, revealed the two pilots, plus a supervisory pilot in the jump seat, were all talking about the company retirement plan changes when the accident occurred. Everyone on board was killed.

I'm not talking about exhaustion (the problem with many long-haul truck drivers) or impairment (drunk driving). I'm talking about a deliberate but often unconscious bias toward doing many things at once with potentially disastrous consequences. We can see this in major corporate decisions, such as acquisitions and divestitures, and in major personal decisions, such as selection of a college or job changes.

We need a positive approach, a rewiring of our brain, guided by a focus on the immediate or priority task at hand. You can't call the computer repair people to fix your brain.

Being Positive Is Not Enough

We need more than mere "happy thoughts." The old "positive mental attitude" of Napoleon Hill and W. Clement Stone are pretty much artifacts of a simplistic age. (Stone made a Fortune worth about $450 million being brilliant in the insurance business. He developed a positive mental attitude *because* he had $450 million, not the other way around. His etiology was mixed up. When Alan told him this, as president of one of his companies, he was promptly fired. His attitude wasn't too good that day!)

Disney has advocated "wishing upon a star." We're told not to be dreamers. Yet we also hear from highly successful entrepreneurs that they've always had a dream. Being a dreamer who dreams of winning the lottery or a job promotion will not, as Captain Picard used to order, "Make it so."

So what is the proper amount of dreaming, aspiring, and visualizing? Gabrielle Oettingen, an NYU psychology professor, has researched the impact of positive thinking and dreaming in term of the aspirations one believes are important. In her book, *Rethinking Positive Thinking*, she concludes that merely thinking good thoughts is not enough to get people motivated sufficiently to act on their dreams, and it may, in fact, be an impediment.[lxi]

She had two student groups engage in an exercise where one group was told to fantasize that the following week would be fantastic for them—great parties, good grades, good health, and so on. The other group was told to simply record their fantasies for the next week, whether they were positive or negative.

Those who fantasized a great week accomplished less, in review of the week's actual activities, than did the other group with more neutral thoughts. Oettingen believes that positive fantasies may create a kind of complacency that "just wishing will make it so." What is actually needed to be able to take positive thoughts *and act on them successfully.*

Hence, when people with positive thoughts were able to identify obstacles in the way of achieving their goals they had a far better chance of acting on their dreams and achieving them. They had to act on the impediments, once identified, and could not be complacent with the mere wish.

Her process is known as WOOP:

Wish. First define your goal, anything from weight loss to landing a new sale.

Outcome. Imagine what the best possible outcome for you is, such as excitement, pleasure, money, recognition, and so forth.

Obstacles. After the dream and outcome, identify the roadblocks to success. What can keep this from happening.

Plan. Now that you know the roadblocks, plan to prevent them from occurring or mitigating their impact if they occur.[lxii]

We'd add a fifth factor to the model to say what are the specific *behaviors* that you can take to put your plan into action.

Try WOOP for yourself. The intent is to help change your thinking patterns in a variety of settings, personal and professional. Try this in a quiet place, and give yourself 15 minutes, letting your fantasies focus on what you truly would like to accomplish:

Table 7.1 WOOP

Wish: What do you want to achieve? Make it challenging but doable in a prescribed time frame.	Outcome: What is the best outcome for this wish that would make a difference in your life?
Obstacle: What is the biggest obstacle that will get in the way of your success? Go ahead and visualize how this problem will stop you.	Plan: What are the best steps you can take to overcome this obstacle. Take a moment to imagine how you can overcome it.
Behaviors: Go ahead and be specific about what behaviors (making a phone call, rewriting your plan) you will do if the obstacle above occurs.	

Source: Rethinking Positive Thinking.

There are two ways to change your life. You can change the way you think and when you do that, you will change your behavior. Or you can change your behavior, and with new successes, you will change your thinking. Gabrielle Oettingen's WOOP process helps us do both. By realistically dreaming about our aspirations *and* targeting specific behaviors to overcome what has kept us from success, we can begin to make those positive dreams a genuine reality.

Finding Your Superpowers

Each of us has uniqueness not shared with others. Call this your "superpowers." Fortunately, no phone booth is necessary for a change of clothing, a la Superman, since phone booths have disappeared, but your superpowers have not.

One of the primary reasons that we don't feel good about ourselves, suffer from low self-worth, and lose resilience is that *we often wind up doing things we're simply not good at doing.* We take on a job, launch a career, engage in a hobby—because someone ordered us to, or suggested it, or because we feel normative pressure. We have to overcome our basic lack of affinity for the endeavor, which is draining and, sometimes, impossible.

The natural antidote is to focus on things we do well, professionally and personally. Just because some parents created a wonderful company doesn't mean the children should be expected to run it. Just because your mother is a dentist doesn't mean you need to be. Most people look absolutely idiotic with their baseball cap on backward, especially when they then shield their eyes from the sun with their hand. But normative pressure forces us into dumb situations if we yield to it. (Think of how those tattoos on Millennials will look in 20 years when they're striving for senior leadership positions or when what was a butterfly has morphed with sagging skin into Godzilla.)

Superpowers are often called merely "strengths." There is a plethora of books on finding your strengths, measuring them, and assessing them, *but often the books assume you're damaged if your "findings" aren't consistent with certain strengths.* They deny your uniqueness and try to drive you back into the herd. They don't advocate your superpowers, they advocate their superpowers.

Case Study

One of my coaching clients, a CFO of a publicly traded company, was a smart fellow whose greatest superpower was that he was a very thoughtful and strategic thinker who could successfully analyze most situations. His greatest weakness was how he dealt with people. He would lose patience with people and get easily aggravated if they did not understand the subject matter he was discussing, which was often about financial matters where they were not nearly as skilled in understanding as he. This caused him and his colleagues a great deal of stress.

In order to help him build his resilience to these kinds of situations, we decided that we would use his superpower of being able to analyze a situation before he approached it to determine exactly how he would deal with the "human side" of the equation. Given these understandings, he could then make some choices around the behaviors he wanted to show to others, such as being a better listener, educating them about the subject matter, or even deciding to delegate the task of a particular meeting to his controller who was better with people than he was.

Using his superpower of "being a great analyzer," this CFO was soon seen by his colleagues as much more supportive and understanding, not as not someone who just created more stress for himself and others.

One of the greatest issues with superpowers is that people won't admit they have them! Too many of us deny that we're really superb at some things, and tend to think that "humility" is some kind of key to the entrance to heaven. (In 30 years of consulting, Alan has never heard a buyer proclaim, "Get me a humble consultant!") I don't want a humble heart surgeon, I want one who believes he walks on water. I don't want a humble athlete with the ball at the key point at the end of the game, I want someone who calls for the ball or wants to be at bat because he or she thinks that's the team's best hope.

Do you "call for the ball"? Your negativity bias may be giving you the message to not go for it just in case you fail. That fear is what often prevents us from admitting to and owning our superpowers.

Here's a simple exercise to focus on superpowers and overcome humility, called "Frame It/Name It/Claim It/Aim It." It's important for better understanding our greatness.

Frame It. What is the context with which you want to use your superpowers. We'll assume it is for good and beyond that is it to achieve some new skill at work or to

_____

_____

Name it. What words or phrases describe some of the things you do well? Consider terms such as intuitive, analytical, empathic, action-oriented, and so forth. What have *others* told you that you do well?

_____

_____

Claim it. Pick one of the superpowers above and provide specific examples of situations where you have employed them effectively. This will help with your recognition in your accomplishments. This is usually the most challenging part of this exercise since most of us are afraid to acknowledge our successes.

_____

_____

_____

_____

Aim it. In what ways can you begin using the superpowers for similar accomplishments tomorrow? Consider how you can help others with some challenge or overcome stressors you are dealing with.

_____

_____

_____

_____

Your superpowers are untapped resources for building resilience. Avoiding the negative and focusing on the positive will build your strengths and drive you right through adversity.

CHAPTER 8

Investing in Yourself: Your Personal Return on Investment

In groundbreaking research, Stanford psychologist Carol Dweck identified that we have control over our negativity bias. Her work on "mindset" showed that we could break out of our perception that we can't affect the world and that we can change this idea, so that we come to see the way we think as something that is flexible and easy to change.[lxiii]

For most of us, this should not come as a surprise. We've all had great successes in our lives. Often we may attribute these to luck or good fortune, but for people who have the right mindset, they recognize that it is due to their hard work and mental attitude.

Having the right mental attitude allows us to think through challenging and stressful times with a target of success *and not just survival.* Developing this attitude can be thought of as a personal investment we make in ourselves, so that we create a great return down the road. Like the investments you might make in your home or retirement plan, seeds planted today can grow exponentially. *Consider how much different your life would be if you decreased the amount of worrying you spent every day on whether or not you were doing okay at your job!*

We'll build a personal formula for success and show ways that you can maximize your return on your resilience investment.

How Do You See the World?

Do you see the world as a terribly challenging place that you cannot master, or do you see the world as offering you an opportunity to master it?

As we've discussed, for most people, the negativity bias has us running scared and protecting the downside of our lives to make sure the worst does not happen. Risk aversion, the tendency to play so that we don't lose rather than going for the win, can become a mindset for ourselves when we live in a fearful way.

We like to ask the question, "What does the evidence show about how successful or how much of a failure your life has actually been?"

There are many measures of success you can use to gauge your life:

- Having a happy marriage or partnership
- Raising healthy kids
- Enjoying your job
- Having sufficient money to have a home, enjoy vacations, and provide for your family
- Reaching a career goal
- Having hobbies that give you satisfaction
- Giving back to your community and philanthropy
- Having good health
- Staying out of trouble
- Sleeping well and being energetic
- Having and implementing good ideas

Each of us has to identify our own measure of what is important in our lives. But each of us has the same goal framed by Thomas Jefferson, "the pursuit of happiness."

Resilience is not just about avoiding stress but finding more joy, ease, and grace in our lives. How can we find it?

Jefferson didn't write about achieving happiness *but pursuing it as if it is an unattainable goal that we seek in an asymptotic manner,* perhaps getting closer and closer but never fully getting there. (Zeno's Paradox states that if you make half the distance to your goal each day, you will never reach it.) Happiness is a relatively recent phenomenon in our culture becoming important only in the past 300 years. It's gone from something that only the luckiest of people possessed to something that we now consider a right. Instant gratification is no longer a pejorative, but an ideal!

In fact, the etymological root of happiness is from the old Norse *Hap* meaning "luck."

There are different ways that people pursue happiness:

- Living a good and virtuous life—doing the right thing all the time according to one's beliefs.
- Smiling, laughing, and enjoying life in the moment.
- Pursuing pleasures that bring you joy, like finding the perfect bottle of wine or building a rocking chair.
- Having financial success and material possessions.
- Experiencing positive events like birthdays, vacations, or seeing friends.
- Finding meaning in one's life through a spiritual practice, providing service, raising a family or through a career; having deep religious convictions.

Each of us must define happiness for ourselves and seek it in our own way. Happiness *is* possible, but first we have to define what that state appears to be, even if we never totally reach it. There is another old saying, "No wind is a good wind if one doesn't know the port of call." We make a mistake when we insist that others find the same happiness that we do. In fact, many of the most successful relationships are based on some pursuits of individual happiness, and some joint.

However, we make a greater mistake when we insist that others, such as our spouse, find the same happiness that we do. Each person must find their own source of happiness, and then, together with their partner, find how to create happiness as a couple.

Happiness Is Possible

In the movie *Forrest Gump*, Lt. Dan is Forrest Gump's squadron commander who is caught up in a firefight during the Vietnam War. Lt. Dan is badly injured during the battle. Forrest saves his life by carrying him out of harm's way, but he loses both his legs. When they meet up in the Army hospital and in several subsequent visits, Lt. Dan is angry and resentful of Gump saving his life. He believed that his destiny and what would be his source of greatest personal happiness would be to die, like his forbearers, on the battlefield. As a double amputee, Lt. Dan became an angry person who viewed himself as worthless, but that did not keep him from continuing to look for happiness in all its ugly and beautiful ways.

At first, Lt. Dan turns to alcohol and drugs living in New York. There is no way we could say Lt. Dan had any happiness during that time, but addiction, which will never lead to happiness, is usually a search by one person to find a path for some joy in his or her life.

As the story progresses, Lt. Dan takes up Forrest's invitation to join him in Louisiana after Forrest became a shrimp boat captain. Dan must have decided there was no happiness to be found in the world of addiction and his drive to find some kind of happiness led him to seek out the life Forrest was offering. He joins the crew of the *Jenny* (it's just Forrest and Dan) and off they go to fish for shrimp, unsuccessfully. Their shrimping struggles continue until they find themselves out to sea when Hurricane Carmen strikes the Louisiana coast. While Forrest is petrified during the storm, Dan uses the experience to once again face life and death demons by sitting on the mast of the shrimp boat and challenging the storm (and his higher power) to bring on all its fury. He is ready to wage war and, in a strange way, seems content to fight this demon that has kept him from finding his own peace of mind.

As the Hurricane ends, Forrest and Dan are on the only shrimp boats left floating. They cash in their good luck to form the biggest shrimp company on the Gulf Coast. They become wealthy men and Dan finally finds a sense of contentment when he obtains a pair of prosthetic legs and a wife to wed. His journey to happiness was long and rocky, but he acknowledges and thanks Forrest for helping him find it.[lxiv]

Lt. Dan showed us the full range of emotional responses to his desperate and emotionally difficult experience. His initial responses showed how posttraumatic stress can overwhelm a person and can lead him or her to consider suicide or other life-destroying behaviors. Yet Dan also demonstrated another device that can be used to build on emotionally challenging situations: ***posttraumatic growth***.

In a *New York Times Magazine* article, Jim Rendon describes the work of Professors Richard Tedeschi and Lawrence Calhoun, from the

University of North Carolina in Charlotte. Their research included interviewing over 600 people who had experienced significant trauma. They began their research by interviewing survivors of trauma: people who had experienced life-threatening illness, loss of children or spouse, or had been a prisoner of war.

Their findings revealed that while everyone wished that the traumatic event had never happened, *most of them recognized that they had learned a new appreciation for life and for their ability to cope with the challenges of their lives.* They called their core findings "posttraumatic growth," in that people grew from these horrific experiences. They identified five common factors that these survivors felt had strengthened them as people:

- An enhanced appreciation for life following the traumatic event.
- Discovering newer and more possibilities for their lives than they had had before the traumatic event.
- A greater sense of personal strength, where they were less willing to settle for things they might have settled for before the traumatic event.
- A greater commitment to building strong relationships with loved ones.
- A greater sense of spiritual fulfillment.[lxv]

It seems reasonable to assume that if people who experienced trauma that we usually associate with the worst of circumstances, can begin to apply some of the principles of posttraumatic growth to their own happiness, then perhaps the rest of us can build in happiness strategies to our everyday emotional stressors that we experience at work and at home. Can we think about building a habit of happiness by adding some easy exercises to our daily routine that can help turn our negative thoughts to more positive ones?

Seven Ways to Beat a Path to Happier Times
1. **Consider what makes you happy**. It seems pretty obvious, but many people do not know what makes them happy. Once you get that in place, your choices become obvious. Don't look to what others define as happiness. Set your own path.

2. **Help others.** Being benevolent to others is a powerful force for happiness. Even small gestures like getting someone a cup of coffee or helping carry packages into work creates joy. The idea of doing a random act of kindness to an unknowing neighbor often brightens up an entire day.

3. **Surround yourself with people who have a positive attitude**. Notice how some people in restaurants are laughing and enjoying each other, whereas at some tables people have their heads buried in their food and are not interacting. Build your own table of happy people in your life, not just when you dine. I've never found people buried in their cell phones or lost in their ear buds while sitting with others to be especially positive people for others.

4. **Appreciate what is right in front of you**. Take a few moments to enjoy being in the moment. Whether it is at work, going for a walk, or talking to your son or daughter, be present to what is happening at that particular time. Ask yourself why this activity matters, and what it means for you.

5. **Challenge yourself.** Set a goal for something you want to achieve every day. It does not have to be big, but should be something that at the end of the day, you can look back and say that you achieved that objective. The most successful people tend to have two or three real priorities every day and pride themselves on achieving them, even if minor matters have to wait. Stop worrying about e-mail. It will still be there later.

6. **Affirm others.** A senior leader told me that he needed to recognize the accomplishments of his team more often. He is using his Outlook calendar to remind himself at 8 a.m. to "recognize someone for his or her good work today." After a month, he told me that his team is doing better and he feels better about their performance. In business, have random breakfasts with a variety of people to elicit their opinions.

7. **Stop it!** We all get negative thoughts and when you do, just tell yourself to stop doing it and focus on something that is working for you. That can change your thinking all around. (I strongly suggest you watch the Bob Newhart classic, brief comedy routine on YouTube where he plays a therapist who cuts to the chase: https://www.youtube.com/watch?v=Ow0lr63y4Mw)

Getting a 10-Bagger

My dad was a stockbroker and I grew up in a house where corporate earning reports were talked about as frequently as the baseball scores and weather. My dad was a student of the markets and during his lifetime he became a master at understanding the trends and behaviors that drove stocks and corporations. He kept daily charts in big loose-leaf binders of hundreds of stocks and used this technical analysis when making recommendations to his clients. Every night he would sit in his office and study these charts looking for trends and tracking the behaviors of these stocks. He was always looking for the next 10-bagger.

In the world of investing, one of the biggest dreams is to have a 10-Bagger an investment you may have made in a stock is worth 10 times its original purchase price. For example, if you bought 100 shares of a stock at $5 and it went to $50, you've got a 10-bagger. In order to nail a 10-bagger, you have to start early, have great insights and vision, and make sure you persist through the ups and downs of a stock's progressions. If you'd have bought Netflix in early 2010 when it was around $10, you would have had a 10-bagger after it did its six-for-one split in 2015 and was trading around $100. During those five years, it had a rocky run, rising and falling as the fortunes of the company ebbed and flowed, until it broke through with its winning series of internally built shows such as *House of Cards* and *Orange is the New Black*.

Here is what the stock chart of a 10-bagger looks like (Figure 8.1):

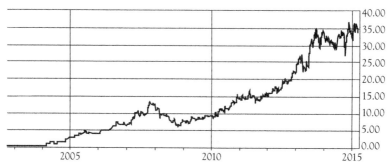

Figure 8.1 10-Bagger

Building your own 10-bagger of success holds some of the same requirements as building a stock 10-bagger: start early to make changes for success, have great insights and visions about your own lifestyle, and persist and show grit to help achieve your goals.

My dad always told me that the fascinating thing about finding the next 10-bagger was that there was no single right way to find it. For him, it was reading the charts of stocks' daily or weekly movements, called "technical analysis." For someone else, it might be more fundamental analysis, where you examine the financial health of a company by looking at accounting ratios and strategic plans. Peter Lynch, who headed the Magellan Fund and is one of the markets most legendary stock pickers, described how he would accompany his wife to the mall, walking around the stores and seeing which store had the biggest crowds. He'd then go back to his office, study the company, and make a call about buying the stock. Great stock investors have a certain approach or mindset about how they evaluate, determine, and decide about buying or selling a stock and they would stick to that method, often having it lead to success.

Having your own mindset about how you approach stress and how to become stress resilient is a central part of the thesis of the *Resilience Advantage*. We can look to different approaches and methods to help us build resilience and put into play winning formulas that will help us successfully cope with our life challenges.

Carol Dweck, the Stanford psychologist mentioned earlier, has researched the idea of how our mental mindset affects resilience for many years. Our mindset can be defined as how we think, or our established set of attitudes and assumptions that we hold about people, places, and things.

Dweck's research has focused on her discovery that the way people think about their mindset can be placed along a continuum ranging from a "fixed mindset" to a "growth mindset."

Her research, based on how children and adults think about certain innate abilities such as their intellect and talents, relates to whether people's mindsets consider that these qualities are fixed and unchanging or whether they can be altered, improved, and strengthened.[lxvi]

People who tend to have more of a fixed mindset believe that their abilities today were completely prewired into their brains and that they cannot do anything to truly improve on them. Their goal is to look as smart and capable as possible and avoid ever seeing themselves as failing.

People with a growth mindset believe that while they were born with certain inherent qualities such as intelligence or personality, they can be intentional about improving and growing. For example, challenging oneself with crossword puzzles or other difficult mental tasks can help build new neuronal brain connections. Growth mindset people see failure as an opportunity to learn and grow and will openly acknowledge how their failures were great learning experiences for them.

Developing a growth mindset means that you are a learner, enjoy learning, and recognize that you can take steps to improve yourself.

Five Ways to Build Your Right Mindset
- **Start with the basics.** Break down the way you currently think about problems, so that you understand what is working and what is not working and then go ahead and make changes. John Wooden, the legendary basketball coach for UCLA, used to start off every season by reviewing with his players how to lace up their sneakers. His thinking was that if their shoes were properly tied, then there would be less chance of them developing blisters during the season. On your job, are the fundamentals in place in terms of relationships, knowing the mission of your company and your department? Are your efforts driving to success?
- **See learning as a journey and not a destination.** People with fixed mindset see an assignment and want to merely reach the criterion point. They have project objectives and want to check off the boxes that they got the job done. With a growth mindset, you are asking, what can I learn from this project that will help me achieve this goal and learn something I can apply down the road? They are constant learners. Are you looking at a task, a job, *or a career?*
- **Call it an "experiment."** If you're not sure how a possible change will work out, be a scientist and find out. When asked how it felt to fail 10,000 times in trying to make a light bulb, Thomas Edison responded, "I didn't fail, I just learned

10,000 ways not to make a light bulb."[lxvii] Winston Churchill said, "Success is never final and failure seldom fatal, it's courage that counts."[lxviii]

- **Rapid prototyping.** We are seeing this approach put into play more and more in business settings. Risk taking is important, and we have to try different ideas to see which gets traction. Alan runs workshops continuously and is fearless about trying something new. He'll put an idea out there and if it does well, great. If not, that's also great. If a workshop works one year but fails to get traction the next, he dumps it and moves on to his next idea.

- **Be inspired and inspire others.** Consider lessons and successes you see in others and decide how you can put their ideas into play. Think about bosses who you have respected and who earned your trust. What did they do and how did they inspire you? Who has written you a thank you note for your contribution to their career? How did you inspire them? Inspiring and being inspired is a sure cue of a growth mindset.

Having a growth or learning mindset is the surest path to the 10-bagger since learning is the great multiplier. Your 10-bagger at work is not that difficult.

Engagement research, which is now standard in most companies, reveals that only 50 percent of employees truly enjoy and get a sense of satisfaction from their work. The remaining 50 percent tolerate their jobs or perhaps even hate going into work. And we know that gratification in work is the primary motivator behind job performance (never money).[lxix]

Finding your heart in the workplace requires both the efforts of the employee and employer to establish the kind of workplace that each party needs.

Salvador Maddi and Deborah Khoshaba's 12-year study of the breakup of Illinois Bell identified three key elements that helped employees thrive through the toughest of workplace challenges, which in their case was the dissolution of their company. Those three elements were:

Table 8.1 Maddi and Khoshaba's Model of Resilience Applied to the Worksite

	Employer	Employee
Commitment	• Be more transparent. • Communicate more. • Create a meaningful work environment where employees understand their role in the corporate mission.	• Find the right job so you can be committed to the work. • Make sure you are using your best talents in your job. • Know your customers so that you can see the results of your efforts.
Control	• Delegate tasks to team members so they can make meaningful contributions. • Provide people with opportunities to customize their work style. • Encourage and allow failure so that people are engaged.	• Ask for more responsibilities or take on a special project that you can own. • Discuss your wins and losses with others so that you understand what you are doing well or not so well. • Ask for work style changes that suit your life, like remote work or a standing desk.
Challenge	• Inspire people to a higher mission in their work. • Demonstrate a genuine concern for their well-being. Know the names of their kids. • Help develop their professional career. Take time to review their strategies for success.	• Look for opportunities to learn at work. • Don't always look for the easy way out. Be willing to take on tough tasks. • Ask for help if you are needing assistance.

Based on: Resilience at Work, Salvadore Maddi and Deborah Khoshaba

- **Commitment**, or an attitude of being involved in what is happening in the workplace rather than just being an observer of events.
- **Control** where the employee is given the opportunity to influence the outcome of their workplace rather than just having to respond to events. (This, colloquially, is "empowerment.")
- Seeing events as **challenges** that can be overcome and learned from rather than seeing them as difficulties that can't be overcome.[lxx]

How do these work for the employee and employer?

Your Personal Stress Resilience IQ

While engineers can successfully calculate stress formulas for all kinds of objects from bridges to airplane wings, calculating a stress formula for people is a little more challenging.

Furthermore, the goal is not about assessing how much stress you can handle (the way most stress assessments are done), but instead to find out what you get out of living a more resilient lifestyle. For that we have developed a formula that will help you maximize the return on investment you receive by working on being a more resilient person and being able to handle your stress more successfully and gracefully.

Here is a shot at a formula for maximizing your return on investment for being resilient-focused:

What is the investment that you have to make to achieve just some of the goals that resilience offers you above?

- **How well have you handled past stressors?**

Probably some good, some not so good, if you are like most of us. Some situations demand different skills. What have been your strategies for addressing stress in the past and what skills do you have that you can use in the future?

- **How well you take care of yourself across the Resilience Continuum?**

Your success in handling previous stressful situations (**A**) +
How well you use the Resilience Continuum to address stress in all circumstances (**B**) −
The Stress Reality (how real and intense your stressor truly is) (**C**) ×
Your attitude of whether you see stress as a threat or challenge (**D**) =
Your Personal Stress Resilience IQ

$$[(A + B) - C] \times D = \text{Your Personal Stress Resilience IQ}$$

This is where all the stories you hear about taking care of yourself, how you plan and prepare, your exercise routine, eating well, meditating or being mindful, getting sufficient rest, and all the other wellness strategies come into play. All the effort at being healthy is about improving our lifestyle, so that we can be ready and armed to effectively address the stress in our lives.

- **How threatening is the stress you are experiencing? Is it dangerous or are you creating a catastrophe that is just not there?**

Having a diagnosis of a life-threatening disease is different from a traffic jam, even though both light up our stress hormones. Carefully weighing out the value of one stressor over another will dramatically drive a positive ROI.

- **Do you see life as a great adventure or something to endure?**

Your mental mindset will help you see the world as a challenge and not a threat and having an abundance mentality versus a poverty mentality will help accelerate your way through adversity.

Maximizing Your Return

By now, you have become familiar with the basic elements of the Resilience Advantage and why having a resilience attitude will help you to take charge of stressful situations instead of allowing them to take charge of you. On our website, **www.theresilienceadvantage.com**, you will find assessment and planning tools that will help you take your actions a step closer to becoming stress resilient. Use the password *resilienceadvantage* to access this material.

CHAPTER 9

Bringing Your Best to Work: Your Daily Dose of Success

I once had a boss who would always say to us during stressful times, "You think work is tough? Why do you think we call it work?"

It's these kinds of comments from bosses that often provoke high levels of stress, frustration, and fatigue among employees. It conforms to the "stress management" model that there is nothing that you, I (as the boss), or the corporation can do to address stress and pressure in the workplace.

Stress in the workplace is real, but it is no greater than stress in life. Surveys that examine people's perception of stress identify personal and work stress *as equal*. In fact, much more research has been done about stress in the workplace. We'll examine the big three workplace stressors—having enough resources to get things done, gaining a sense of control over what you do, and having meaning in your work. We'll explore ways that you can use these opportunities to help you find more satisfaction and sense of accomplishment and reward from your workplace.

For many companies, the ideas and activities for "resilience" are already firmly entrenched in their culture and workplace. For IT professionals, resilience is a process that ensures that all the data is backed up and secure. For operational leaders, resilience means they've carefully measured "risk" events, such as fires, earthquakes, or tornadoes, and assessed their potential impact on operational costs.

As we've discussed previously, engagement research shows that roughly 50 percent of the workforce basically just wants to go to work, do their job, and then head home at the end of the day. If you are part of the 50 percent that wants to get more and give more at work, then resilience can help you build a plan for workplace success.

This is One Crazy Workplace

I was sitting outside my boss's office awaiting his return from a meeting. It was our regular, weekly meeting and I had come in with my agenda for our discussion. John liked having an agenda for our meeting even if we rarely stuck to it.

As usual, John was running a bit late, but I heard him walking down the hall, barking orders to my colleagues as he walked along the executives' offices.

"Susan, rerun the schedule on that software implementation. We're going to have to speed it up."

"Tony, I'm getting pushback on the sales figures you estimated, David doesn't believe them. I need more backup on those."

Two down I thought, I wonder who is next and what's coming my way? Right next to his office sat our chief operating officer. On his way to our meeting, John stepped into Deb's office and told her "Deb, you won't believe this but the boss's wife called our call center yesterday for some information and it took us 60 seconds to answer the call. He is quite upset and you better do something about it!"

A few moments later, John made it to our meeting and acted more exhausted than angry. Despite our appointment, I could see that my work was not on his radar, as he had just come from meeting with his boss, our corporate CEO, and it apparently was not pleasant. As often happened to me with different bosses over my career, our division CEO turned to me and said, "It's a good thing you're a psychologist, anything I say to you, you have to keep to yourself." While not exactly true, since we don't have that kind of professional relationship, I understood what he was saying. "I need some place and someone to vent to."

John went on to describe how much stress he endures. It's not only that the responsibility of running our division was a day-to-day challenge with all the business, personnel, and regulatory challenges that he had to face, but that the pressures that he experienced from his boss and board were enormous. "As you can no doubt tell, I was in a meeting today with David (our corporate CEO) and he really let me have it."

Of course, all the business questions went on for the entire hour, but when he capped it off with the CEO's wife's wait time experience, that just about put us over the top: "It's a good thing, his office is on the second floor. If I had decided to jump, I'd have only suffered a few broken bones."

That brought about a little chuckle and with that, his venting over, he was feeling better. "Thanks, for listening," he said. "Now what is on your agenda?"

The workplace is crazy these days, from top to bottom. I've seen it over and over again. In meetings with clients and in discussions with colleagues, everyone has the same feeling that their company is misfiring on some cylinders. Clients tell me that their company is running so inefficiently that they must have the worst "operations," "strategy," and "leadership" (name your function) of any company around. Even when you read reviews on so-called great companies like Google and Apple on websites like Glassdoor, negative comments appear from people who are frustrated, dismayed, and disappointed about how their workplace has seemed to fail them in providing a successful and rewarding work experience. Recently, a scathing *New York Times* report on Amazon called it a bruising workplace, one where it might be possible to see your colleague "practically combust."[lxxii]

My takeaway from that meeting was the enormity of the challenges being faced in organizations across all levels. In the olden days, it used to be thought that the boss had it easy and could just order folks around and make things happen. In stress terms, the boss was often considered to be a stress *carrier*. He (and it was usually he) didn't necessarily have symptoms of stress, but instead conveyed stress to everyone else. Today, we see that everyone in the organization is under the gun, just hoping to come up with some kind of remedy to whatever situation they are dealing with that day.

The good news is that the perceptions we all share about the workplace are common and even have a name. The acronym VUCA, meaning Volatile, Uncertain, Complex, and Ambiguous, represents the current state of how the workplace is experienced by most of us and is probably more explanatory than the idea that our workplaces are in disarray.

- **Volatility** means that your day may be punctuated by unexpected or unstable events that have to be addressed, usually immediately. It's the speed of events that throw you and your organization for a loop. It's the phone call you get from a client requesting a change in shipments or your boss telling you to drop whatever you are working on to complete the report that was due next month.

- **Uncertainty** translates to events that you cannot predict and that might be thrust upon you without providing you much time to react. A government agency releases new guidelines that will change the way you are able to price your product. Many organizations have to find lines of credit to continue their work when our dysfunctional Congress and state legislators are unable to do their job and complete a budget.

- **Complexity** is one of the greatest challenges for all of us, as it presents a myriad of interconnected parts and variables. Our efforts to simplify complex problems become difficult, because we are not sure which factors are most critical. All of us experience the challenge of learning new software for our personal computers. When we look at corporate implementations of systems like SAP or Oracle most of the time we let out a collective groan. Implementation teams try to make the process straightforward and simple, but there are usually just too many factors and the more options we have *the less likely we are to make quick, high-quality, confident decisions.*

- **Ambiguity** is one of the newest characteristics that has entered the workplace and, for that matter, our lives. Ambiguity relates to not having enough information (or, sometimes, perhaps too much information in order to be able to make a clear decision. Working in matrixed organizations creates a great deal of ambiguity, as it may be uncertain to whom an employee can turn for decisions or even they should be seeking to resolve complex issues. (And people can "hide" from accountability much more easily.)

This is the current workplace for many of us. It may not be like this every day, but many days as information pours into our workplace, we are often faced with what may seem like a "fog of work," a feeling that we can't see our way through the VUCA of our work situation. The former world heavyweight champion, Mike Tyson, summed it up beautifully in one of his most famous quotes, "Everybody has a plan until they get hit in the jaw. Then, like a rat, they stop in fear and freeze."[lxxiii]

Sounds a lot like the stress reaction happens pretty easily and regularly in our workplaces.

Forget about Balance and Build Agility

During a consultation with a group of teams focused on innovation at the British Standards Institute, the managing director came down from London to listen to the presentations. At the conclusion of several hours of ideas he said, "If these are such bloody good ideas, why hasn't anyone already thought of them?" That ended that. (To this day, he is one of the three worst executives I've ever encountered.)

Not every manager misses the point of how much most employees want to contribute to the success of their company, or that they are not at all afraid of work and effort. In fact, many companies are recognizing that the workplace has gone from challenging to invidious and has come up with a variety of "life/work" or "work/life" ideas that are designed to help employees balance their lives.

Netflix now offers a year of parental leave for new parents. Colgate Palmolive has a backup childcare center for employee's kids. The grocery store chain Wegmans provides flexible part-time scheduling for college students and other employees. Google encourages employees to spend time working on projects of their own ideas that may help advance the Google mission. Many perks are out there to help employees, including telecommuting, flex time schedules, tuition reimbursement, and, of course, vacation time, something that many Americans do not even fully use.

What companies have to offer is hardly the issue, however. The real question is what we as employees do with these perks and how we use them. What companies hope for is that their employees use these benefits to stay balanced in their lives and that they recognize that the company is concerned about their well-being. To that end, the company hopes that their efforts will increase their employees' commitment or engagement with the organization.

This issue of work/life or life/work balance is a tricky one for most of us. Even though we advocate the idea of balance between work and home, most of us don't execute it very well. Many employees don't take advantage of the benefits they already have. A recent Harris Interactive poll completed for Glassdoor showed that only half of us use the eligible paid vacation and paid time off we've accrued. For those who do get away, six of ten of us work while hanging out at the beach.[lxxiv] LinkedIn recently announced unlimited vacation time for their employees. No doubt, they are confident that it won't be abused. Their records probably show that most employees don't take their already assigned vacation days. Perhaps they think that with unlimited vacation time, employees may take even less than before.

Even other benefits that may help make our lives more balanced are usually not used. Employees may be concerned about how it will look to their boss or colleagues if they are not in the office or may not even know the benefits exist or use them effectively. For example, just 53 percent of employees are enrolled in a retirement plan at work, and wellness programs usually engage 10 percent or less of a company workforce.

We really don't have two lives (a work life and a home life), but instead just one life that we seek to balance throughout all of our activities. It's tempting to suggest people not check their smartphone at night to see if they have an e-mail from their manager, but most of us want to know if there is a work issue, because we care about our work and want to stay on top of it. We want to make sure that we don't fall too far behind and then feel overwhelmed when we check in at the office, which sounds a lot like a "preparatory" resilience strategy. The idea of not bringing work home on the weekend is great, but if there is an important project that needs to get done for next week, then we want to make sure it gets done, because contributing to the success of our organization is important to us and so is our sense of accomplishment.

In the same respect, I would expect employees to take time during the day to make a hotel reservation for their trip to Disney World, skip out early to catch their son's baseball game, or check on the status of their Christmas delivery packages.

Perhaps we can accept that we have only one life and we can create a goal to find a balance between work and home. In fact, this self-imposed battle may be contributing to some of the stress, pressure, and aggravation we experience at work. *Perhaps the question to ask is, how can we bridge these two life activities in a graceful and easy manner, so that we can flow between the two?*

The answer may lie in our ability to be agile.

If we consider the antidote to VUCA and our ability to blend our lives together, then the word that comes to mind is "agility." Agility is the ability to sense and respond to changes in the world around us and to take actions that are fast, focused, and can be done in a flexible manner.

Developing agility also provides an important component in building resilience. People who are agile look for challenging situations, confront them using an array of strategies, and grow from those experiences, so that they can handle future challenges more effectively.

Research has shown that people who possess agile qualities, such as being self-aware and able to think through complex problems, can work effectively with different people and have an ability to create and manage change successfully.

Robert Eichenger, David Lombardo, Victoria Swisher and their team at the consulting firm Korn Ferry have studied what competencies make people successful in the workplace. Their research in learning agility identified five key areas that successful people master which allows them to successfully address complex work situations:

- **Possessing self-awareness,** which includes being committed to learning, being able to manage emotions effectively, and being able to give and receive feedback.
- **Being mentally agile,** which translates to being inquisitive, being able to connect disparate ideas, and not breaking down when facing uncertain events, but rather relishing in them.
- **Dealing with people effectively,** which means you are a highly effective communicator, can deal with conflict well, and can help others succeed.
- Agile people must be able to **handle change successfully** and so are always looking for ways to improve through experimentation. Being a continuous improver helps ensure success in change agility.

- All this doesn't matter if you are not **results agile,** meaning that you are not able to deliver when things are tough or that you lack the resourcefulness to find solutions to problems when others cannot.[lxxv]

Developing agility is an area where organizations can make a specific and intentional effort to help their employees build these skills, allowing them to address stressful and complex situations more effectively. Lt. Colonel Chris Gehler of the US Army War College wrote about the importance of institutions supporting the learning of agility. Being intentional in this learning through accelerated and experiential efforts helps the participant to understand and integrate new skills for immediate use. [lxxvi]

Of course, the US military is a strong proponent of agility. We've seen how today's soldiers are not just warriors, but also negotiators, community builders, and educators. This ability to adapt to different workplace requirements demands a skill set that precludes getting angry, frustrated, and stressed, and instead requires reflection, seeing the big picture and situational flexibility. These skills or competencies build and enhance agility and our performance and also strengthen our ability to be resilient in stressful situations.

Sheetz is a privately held chain of convenience stores located across the eastern and southeastern United States, with over 450 store locations, employing more than 13,000 individuals in retail locations, distribution centers, and corporate offices. The company plans to grow to more than 1,000 locations. They recognized that in order to do so, they needed to identify and develop their young and upcoming leaders. With the endorsement of senior leadership, they embarked on a program to build agility skills into these leaders.

The development project involved over 50 high-potential future leaders, identified as being exceptional performers. Each leader was assigned to a team and each team was tasked with a specific real-life project that was critical to the Sheetz growth strategy. Project topics included, for example, how well Sheetz "Executes on Projects and Decision Making" and how strong the company was in "Filling the Talent Bench" and "Building Innovative Leadership." Each team was expected to research Sheetz's current practices, seek out best practices, and build a business case for how the company can become best in class, so that it would contribute to their overall growth strategy.

In addition, each team member was asked to identify a specific agility competency that they would be developing for their own professional advancement. Their development plan was to include agility skills that would help them in their job, were in an area in which they did not know much, and were challenging to them. Furthermore, we wanted to make sure the skill acquisition exercise created some stress or "developmental heat," so that their learning was challenging and not just easy.

One of our participants, Dave, took on the challenge to see how he could be less of a perfectionist. In his job, it was important to do things near perfectly, but since work situations rarely have perfect outcomes, he would often find himself frustrated and upset. He described his stress level as "through the roof," and this often translated down to his team. His agility development plan, endorsed and encouraged by his boss, was to focus on being more of an "experimenter," which fell in the change agility category of development.

For Dave, this meant that he had to begin to look at mistakes and errors as something that was perfectly normal. In fact he had to realize that errors were natural and expected at times. He developed a process that documented failures for his team and allowed the team to discuss, learn, and then capitalize on the failures for future learning.

At the conclusion of the project, Dave admitted that this learning opportunity was a breakthrough experience. Not only had he helped his team and company change the way they looked at problems, but he himself was feeling more at ease and less stressed about having to do everything right.

This project lasted over nine months and provided the senior leadership at Sheetz with over 50 different recommendations on how to build novel strategies into their long-term growth plan. Additionally, their next generation of leaders strengthened key agility skills and, perhaps most importantly, learned about how to use these learnings to increase their personal effectiveness in the workplace.

Agility as a component of resilience is surely an antidote to VUCA and workplace stress.

Your Workplace Knows a Lot About Agility

If there is one environment that knows a great deal about resilience, it is your workplace. In fact, one of the most important aspects of business discussed in the C-Suite and boardroom is resilience. As we've discussed before, much of this came about as a result of high impact events like the 9/11 and Katrina tragedies, but technology and the need to secure vital work systems created a resilience approach to business operations. Businesses primarily focus on three key areas of resilience management that include security, IT operations, and business continuity. We'll discuss these a bit more below.

There is hardly any place we can go today where we are not subject to additional security scrutiny. While we all may have concerns about whether or not Big Brother is watching us and whether our privacy is being invaded, we can all probably agree that providing safety to the homeland and our workplaces may be a fair trade-off. This approach to addressing dangerous situations is a cornerstone of security prevention and sounds a lot like the preparation and hardiness model of our Resilience Continuum. Furthermore, when something bad happens, law enforcement's greater coordination means that resources can be mobilized in real-time to get first responders on the scene immediately, improving how crises are handled or what we refer to as navigating stressful situations in real time.

Remember the old Saturday Night Live routine about "Nick, Your Company's Computer Guy?" Nick used to go around driving everyone crazy because they didn't know the correct keystroke to access the company's intranet. Well, today, Nick may be Nora and she may be nuts about IT backup, hacking, and corporate espionage. She's gone beyond hoping that you remember your password to access your files and instead is determined to stop some Russian oligarch from transferring next week's payroll into rubles. Consider the impact of the hack on Target in 2013 and the loss of trust among customers. Target's stock share lost almost 30 percent of its value following the discovery of the theft of over 70 million customer credit cards with a 46-percent drop in its quarterly profits year over the year, along with the CEO's resignation.[lxxvii] When Anthem Blue Cross was hacked in February

2015, over 80 million medical records were stolen. It was not so much the medical information the hackers were seeking, but the customer demographics that included social security numbers, addresses, and employment information. Amazingly, Anthem's IT department did not use any form of encryption for securing social security numbers, so that information was there for the taking. The costs of that hack ran well over $100 million.[lxxviii] For IT professionals, their discussions about resilience focus on maintaining 99.9 percent uptime, keeping the bad guys out, and making sure you keep your password up to date and something only you can "ReL82."

The final aspect of resilience in your workplace is redundancy. Financial service organizations like your credit card company take thousands of calls every day from their customers. Most of these companies maintain a number of call centers. They are constantly evaluating call flow and making sure that calls are answered within a short time frame known as "call answer time." They succeed in meeting their metric by routing calls to difference locations based on the volume of calls at any one center. This resilience focus on redundancy ensures they have sufficiently staffed resources to handle the volume of calls. Redundancy is a critical component of an organization's resiliency.

The Workplace Freakout:
Your Three Big Workplace Stressors

If the workplace knows so much about resilience to organizational stress, why aren't we able to apply resilience strategies to people in the same way we can apply it to corporate operational processes?

The level of stress in the workplace is one of those things that everybody knows about, likes to complain about, feels bad about how it isn't dealt with, and uses as an excuse for not doing well. The failure to properly address this is another example of our inability to manage the stress in our lives.

In the workplace, however there is another reason why stress is not discussed. Everyone is afraid to talk about it.

We know that VUCA is creating a shifting workplace where stability and certainty are out the window, but the lack of discussion about the impact of stress goes even deeper. For employees, complaining too much about stress levels begins to look as if they are not able to handle the workload and that they may wind up being viewed as less than stellar performers. For managers, discussing stress means that they are acknowledging the challenging nature of the workplace and don't know what to do about it. For C-Suite leaders, despite their heartfelt message that "our people are our most important resource," market forces demand that revenues increase and profits grow. Damn the torpedoes, full speed ahead.

There are three big areas that create the greatest sense of stress for most people in the workplace. These include:

1. The sense that you don't have *sufficient resources* to get your job done. This usually leads to frustration and futility.
2. You don't have *control* over your workday and mostly put out fires just trying to keep things even, instead of trying to advance your work successfully.
3. There is a lack of *meaning* to your work, leading you to feel like you are an automaton instead of a creative, committed employee.

Let's examine these in a bit more detail and provide some strategies for dealing with them.

1. **The lack of resources** in getting your job done is a common tale I hear from corporate employees from top to bottom. It is mostly expressed as, "I don't have enough time to get all my work done." Or, "It's ridiculous how much work they expect me to get done around here, we need to hire more people." The key lack of resource, of course, is time and our perception that the demands of our work significantly exceed the resources we have available. Resource limitations are rarely technological or physical, although having the right software to do the job is essential and having a workspace that can facilitate creativity, focus, and collaboration is a big plus. The real key, however, is to work to balance demands and capabilities. This action is within your hands in terms of not only how you manage your own work but also how you want to promote a resource-rich workspace. Here are some ideas to try out:

a. **Get the big picture.** Make sure you have a perspective on how your work and role fits into the larger mission of your company and department. When I work with teams, I make sure they have their own mission statement and that everyone understands their role in that mission, as well as the larger corporate mission. Go ahead and post your mission in some location where you can see it everyday.

b. **Clarify your priorities in writing.** Build your own mission statement by reviewing your job description and performance review. Draft your document on what you believe are the key aspects of your role.

c. **Clarify these priorities with your boss.** Share your document with her and seek agreement about what needs to get done in what order. In a later section for managers, we'll be discussing the "Speed, Quality, and Cost Relationship" and you'll want to check that out for yourself.

d. **Do a time study for one week.** Track how you spend your time during one-week period and see how your actual work matches up against your professed priorities. You'll find that interesting.

e. **Say "No."** One of the most difficult tasks is to say no to co-workers or even a manager who needs help or wants you to attend meetings. Refer back to your mission and priorities and explain how you and your manager have established priorities. If people insist and you feel you must attend, then recognize that this time demand will impact your ability to get other work done. If you attend poorly run meetings, speak to the person in charge of the meeting and ask them to work to improve meeting efficiency.

f. **Reset your calendar to make sure it matches up to those priorities.** In today's world, it is easy to get distracted by the multiple events we are balancing along with keeping track of our online activities. Establishing your calendar so it reflects your priorities can help you get a handle on how your time is spent.

g. **Give yourself permission to not be perfect.** Not all of your work will get done, and you can decide what work is less critical and does not need to get done at 100 percent. In many cases,

80 percent is good enough and some things may just have to get done. In many situations, your level of quality will be much higher than other's expectations.

h. **Create a stimulant rich workplace.** Encourage your organization to create "huddle rooms" and open spaces where you can meet with others outside of a formal meeting. Getting out of familiar settings stimulates thinking and allows for new ideas to be generated.

2. **Having a sense of control** is one of the key factors for being resilient in your workplace (and everywhere else). Knowing that you can take action and that your efforts will yield results is very satisfying. Not having a sense of control over your environment is what creates the feeling of victimization that is so much a part of trying to manage stress. The vicissitudes of your boss's moods, project interruptions, change orders, and family demands that create vagaries in our routines all contribute to our wanting to throw our hands up in the air and hope the wind just takes us away. After all, we have no control anyway. Perhaps, however, there are a few actions to consider:

a. **Shift your focus** from what you can't control to what you can control. Waiting at a client's office, I received a phone call from him. He sounded frantic about the fact that he was not going to make it back to his office for our meeting. He got held up at another meeting and it would now take him 30 minutes to get back. I told him it was okay, to take a deep breath and that we would do our meeting by phone. I could hear the release of tension in his voice as he shifted his focus from frantic to relief.

b. **Aim small, miss small.** In the movie *The Patriot,* Mel Gibson plays the role of the legendary American Revolutionary war hero General Francis Marion, who was known during that time and afterward as the Swamp Fox. In one scene, he wants to ambush a group of British Redcoats, after they have burned down his house and arrested his son for being a spy (which he was). Marion engages the help of his two young sons, who are barely teenagers, to ambush the Redcoats. As they nervously wait for the British to march down the trail to where they are staked out, he reminds them of what he has taught them about shooting a musket, "aim small, miss small," meaning that if they just target a small area, such as a shiny button but miss the button, they'll still hit the target.[lxxix] Translation for gaining control: Shoot for smaller goals for yourself and your work. If you don't hit the mark exactly, you'll still be making progress.

c. **It's not all about you.** One of the mysterious aspects of a lack of control is that we often attribute it to something we are doing wrong. Oftentimes your sense of things being out of your control is accurate and things are, in fact, out of control and have nothing to do with you. Working on one project and then having your boss come and tell you to do something different perfectly describes a situation where your feelings of being out of control are correct.

d. **Seek and provide more information:** Recently I boarded a flight back home on American Airlines, when the pilot announced a mechanical problem and alerted us that we would have to de-plane. Everyone was disappointed, but the pilot and the gate agent did an amazing job of keeping us informed every 15 minutes or so of the status of our flight. We wound up having a three-hour delay until a new plane was flown in, but everyone at the gate stayed in a great mood since we knew what was happening. I sent a note of appreciation to the airline, complimenting the actions of both these great staff members.

e. **Delegate.** You are not in charge of the world, nor are you responsible for getting everything done. You have others on your team, including colleagues, kids, assistants, spouses, friends, and moms and dads. It is okay to ask others for help. Getting some things off your plate increases your confidence about being in control.

3. **Having meaning in your work.** Remember how excited you were when you heard that you landed the job that you currently hold. While it may seem like the company was choosing you, you were also actually choosing that company. Your decision to go with that company was in some measure related to the meaning and purpose of the company. One of the most important factors in work

satisfaction and in our ability to persevere through adversity is to believe that our efforts are making a difference. Think about your favorite sports team and how their mission is always greater than any one player's efforts. Going for a Super Bowl trophy or World Series win helps professional athletes persevere through the pain and persistence required in their careers. If you've lost that sense of mission in your work, here are some things to try out.

a. **Align ideals.** As we discussed earlier, making sure that you are doing work you believe in is important. No matter whom I talk with, whether it is manufacturing specialists who work on a plant floor, marketing professionals, or C-Suite leaders, I always inquire about how their work efforts support and match the business services they are providing to their customers. Then we work toward alignment between the two.

b. **Talk the talk.** As a psychologist, people often ask me to explain why people behave a certain way. Is it their upbringing or personality or something their mother did or didn't do? While I know all these factors are important, I am more interested in how people behave, rather than necessarily understanding the why of their actions. In that regard, by speaking well of your work, looking for the good in what others are doing, and avoiding gossiping and negative, disparaging comments, anyone can begin to create a more meaningful relationship with their work. If you find that you can't get away from acting in a negative way toward your job and employer, it's probably a pretty good sign that it's time for you to move on.

c. **Job Craft your job.** If you are feeling like your work has lost its focus, consider Job Crafting. Developed by the University of Michigan Center for Positive Organizations, job crafting helps you redesign your job based on your strengths and values while meeting the needs of the organization, resulting in a sense of greater engagement and focus, both an essential aspect of being resilient in the workplace.[lxxx]

d. **See how your efforts make a difference.** Adam Grant, a professor at Wharton, asked alumni who had benefited from scholarships to come and speak to undergraduate students who were serving as phone solicitors seeking donations to the University. The student solicitors heard stories of how grateful these alums were for their scholarships and what a difference their education had made in their lives. Following these discussions, the student phone solicitors got back on the phone reaching out for donations to their University. In his research report, Grant determined that the amount of money the students raised with their new solicitation effort increased 171 percent. Meeting the people who were impacted by their labor helped bring the purpose of their work home to them.[lxxxii]

e. **Look for challenges in your work.** Adam Smith, one of the first economists, wrote over 250 years ago that it is man's nature to "live as much at ease as he can." This idea has shaped much of our thinking about why work is something we should avoid and minimize as opposed to embracing and enjoying it. Barry Schwartz, in an article in the *New York Times,* challenges that thinking and suggests that by finding meaning in our work and looking for the challenges that make work rewarding, we can move away from the mindset that work is drudgery and instead see it as a time of learning, rewards, and bringing value and beauty to the world.[lxxxiii]

The Leader's Role In Building Resilience

I hope that by now, you, as a business leader, understand the importance of creating a resilient workforce. Just to be clear, however, let's directly address some of the benefits of resilience from the leader's perspective and what you can do to promote resilience in your workplace.

Since we emphasize stress resilience in this book, it can be easy to think that we are talking about resilience from a health/benefit perspective, while there is some truth in that aspect, thinking about resilience as a workplace performance strategy will be a much more effective approach for you as a leader to integrate into your workplace, both for yourself and for your team.

We've discussed many facets of resilience in this book, but let's simplify the benefits of seeing resilience as a critical competency for you to develop in your team:

- **See the big picture.** The preparation aspect of resilience supports your team in understanding what the business is about and how to plan effectively to make sure that goals are met. By establishing that mindset and providing the tools to do the job (building hardiness), team members gain a new level of confidence in your leadership. Additionally, I hear from many Millennials and Gen Xers that they want to know more about corporate strategy and how their link in the chain contributes to the success of the company.

- **Establish the right priorities.** Unlike the stress management model that creates panic and distress, resilience helps us stay calm. We know we will get through the challenge, since that has been our track record over the year. People don't sweat the small stuff, since they recognize that "stuff happens" and that you want to go with the flow rather than get lost in the swirl. If the IT system is down, people don't walk around bemoaning it, they just move onto the next task until it is back up.

- **Fight the victim mentality.** Employee concerns are legitimate. When employees embrace their own resilience, they are better able to differentiate what the real problems are, and decrease the numbers of grumbles, gripes, and complaints. What can they roll with—and what should they stand up and speak for—becomes clearer to them. You, as a leader, are better able to distinguish between the mundane and the important.

- **Find their power.** Negativity is toxic in the workplace. While resilience will not eliminate it, it will encourage your people to take greater responsibility for what they can do. Team and self-reliance are built into resilience, and help people to take charge of what they can do on their own and with their team.

Team members together should ask, "What can we do to make this workplace better?"

- **Ability to respond and adapt.** Overcoming difficulties is an everyday occurrence and change is the new normal. Your resilient team members roll with these challenges and recognize that this new reality is a part of their workplace. Resilience gives permission to try out new ideas and see how they work, creating an environment where sticking to the old ways of doing things just doesn't work anymore.

- **The learning perspective.** Victories happen and so do failures. Resilience helps with both. Celebrating success is central to resilience strategies as it helps build hardiness and confidence for people that they can do more and more. Conversely, when failure happens, resilience helps your team accept the failure and, more importantly, ask the question, what can we do better? There is decreased moping and blaming of others for why something didn't work. The focus is on how to do it better next time.

- **A more competitive workforce.** I wasn't surprised to find out that the CEO of a 25,000-employee company regularly receives e-mails from customers with concerns about the tenor of her sales force's approach. Seems like they are understaffed, have unrealistic quotas, and work long hours. Not only was her customer service hurting but her sales team turnover rate was high. As we discussed the situation, I pointed out this was a good opportunity for her to embrace "what was not working" and determine what actions she could take. Recognizing that she had to do something about the situation, she began to listen not only to her customers but also to her employees. Seeing that their concerns were legitimate, she was able to change course, invest in a larger workforce with more realistic goals, improving her customer and employee satisfaction rate. Her ability to turn the situation around led her staff to feel more confidence in her as a leader.

- **Healthier people.** You, as a leader, are concerned about the well-being of your people. Research shows that employees are more engaged when they know that their leader knows about and cares about them as people. For you, building a resilience culture not only shows the care you have for your people but that you can also use their failure to be resilient as a barometer of workload and task assignments. As we've discussed, stress is one of the most prevalent concerns in the workplace and is also one of the most taboo topics to discuss. By using the resilience framework, you provide a model for your employees about how to address stress, and more importantly, how to help them to take better care of themselves.

Hence, understanding about the benefits of resilience is part of the equation. So now what can you do about it?

As a leader, there are three key actions that you can take to create a more resilient workplace. We'll use the Resilience Continuum to build our strategy for you as a leader.

1. **Building hardiness and preparation.** As a leader, you control much of what happens in your workplace. You are able to set the stage for building resilience, but these changes listed below will require time to put in place as they demand as much change from you as they do your employees. Think of these actions as helping create a cultural shift in your business.

    a. A hardiness in built when employees are able to:
        i. **Make decisions.** If you micromanage your people, you are actually encouraging victimization among your staff, and are giving them permission to blame you when things don't work out. Furthermore, you are limiting your own career by not acting as a leader, but continuing to serve in the role of an individual contributor by insisting that you do everything.
        ii. **Be involved and committed** to the mission of the organization. When we meet with workplace teams, we often ask, what is their mission? The results usually show that less than

50 percent of team members accurately describe the mission of the organization and their workgroup. By ensuring that your team agrees on their mission and that you regularly review it with them, you help gain their commitment to your company's goals.

iii. **Challenge.** In our work in leadership development, we are constantly forwarding the idea that "developmental heat" is essential for growth. If you give people work that they already know how to do, they soon begin to lose skills, just as you lose muscle if you don't continue to push forward on your workouts. Challenging and then rewarding people for their success (or failure) builds their hardiness for the next challenge.

b. **Workload planning.** You as a leader understand that workload concerns are real, since you are probably working during your weekend to get everything done yourself. While workload volume will probably not decrease, workplace efficiency action will help show that you are genuine about addressing the issue. Some actions include:

   i. **Involve your team** in evaluating the workload. Ask them about where there are inefficiencies and what their ideas are for improving workflows and processes.

  ii. **Critical workload questions.** When I worked in health care, we used to say that there are three key factors related to care delivery: access, cost, and quality. After pointing these out, we would quickly add that you could have any two. "Pick'em," we would say. Of course, we would always go on to address all areas, but recognized that compromise was necessary between all three of these areas. In looking at managing workplace volume, choices also have to be made and typically focus on three critical issues, including:

    1. How **quickly** does this project need to be completed which translates to speed?

    2. What **cost** must be assigned to the project including staff and materials that will drive project success?

    3. What is the **quality** level that is demanded of this project for it to be viewed as successful?

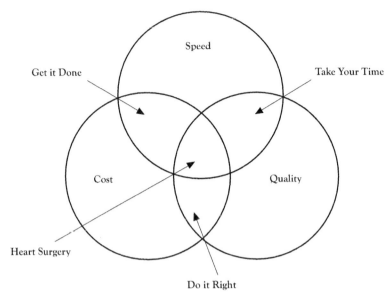

Figure 9.1 *Relationship between Speed, Quality and Cost*

Not all three can be done at 100 percent, given workplace reality. Perhaps the job time frame can be shifted or doing the job at 85 percent will be good enough. Evaluating where your group can create efficiencies by emphasizing key aspects or eliminating unneeded components will help manage the load. The picture above shows the relationship between these three. Unless you are doing heart surgery, you probably don't need to have the perfection of doing all of them perfectly.

c. **Build team effectiveness.** Not every work group needs to operate as a team. Earlier, we said that many teams act as committees and that could be okay for some work groups. For others, however, teamwork is essential to get things done effectively. The distinction is that committees are groups of people who come together, report their wins and losses, and then go back to their offices to figure out their next steps. Teams are different in that they have a common thrust or focus on mission, manifest trust, have the right people in the right roles, work together effectively through conflict and decision making and deliver a great product. Building real and effective teams can be a massive step toward a resilient workforce.

2. **Navigation.** Addressing resilience building in real time is probably the place where you will find the greatest and quickest return on your efforts. While changing employee "stress attitudes" will take time, seeing your efforts to address the issue will definitely get their attention:

    a. **Teach work skills.** When I was a young professional, one of my managers had a session he called "bread crumbs," where his staff got together over a lunch hour to discuss workplace and life issues. In these sessions, we discussed books and articles about our work area, shared tips about Excel or PowerPoint. As our trust level grew, we began to share concerns and challenges that we did not know how to address. Taking time to develop your people will go a long way to helping them get out of the stress victim mentality. Don't assume they know everything about their job.

    b. **Build energy levels**

        i. Shorten meetings to essential "to-dos" rather than mere reporting. Consider 15- or 30-minute meetings. There is nothing sacred about 60 minutes.

        ii. If you have longer meetings, insist on breaks every 90 minutes. Concentration levels fall after that amount of time and people need to move around.

        iii. Try out other meeting formats, such as a walking meeting and creating workspaces in your office for more informal work gatherings.

        iv. Encourage staff to take lunch breaks and to get away from their work for periods of time.

        v. Ask your staff about whether they are using their time for the best and highest service to their role and the needs of the company. There will be some percentage of time that requires grunt work, but you as their manager want to make sure that a significant part of their time uses their best skills in service to the mission.

    c. **Develop focusing capabilities.** There is just way too much information forced upon us. Deciding what is important and what is not important is critical for workplace success. As a leader, you can take on the role of building these capabilities, so that you and your team are on the same page. Examples of these include:

    i. **Identify your process for decision-making.** Ask the question, "Who decides who decides?" When can a staff member make the call on something that needs to be done and when is it your call?

    ii. **Scenario plan.** When we consult and help companies build strategy plans, we have an exercise called "protect the plan," which is designed to recognize how our planning efforts can go awry. We keep that part of our plan in front of us and when there is a derailment, we can help get ourselves back on our feet rapidly.

    iii. **Teach mindfulness.** We've discussed mindfulness in earlier sections of this book. Using mindfulness exercises, such as visioning exercises, can help your team think through in a calm and relaxed manner how to deal with critical real-time issues. If you take us up on a walking meeting (as Aristotle, Steve Jobs, and Harry Truman used to do) you'll probably find a more mindful approach being taken to your areas of discussion.

3. **Recovery and bouncing forward.** Providing space for your staff members (and yourself) to recover from the pressures of work is a great opportunity to demonstrate your commitment to resilience while helping your team be able to do their work in a more effortless manner.

    a. **Provide rewards and recognition.** Barbara Fredrickson, researcher at the University of North Carolina at Chapel Hill, reported that a positive-to-negative ratio (about 3:1) of comments to individuals provides the opportunity for those employees to flourish in their work.[lxxxiv] Recognition is vital and provides a quick and easy tool for boosting spirits and energy. Recognition can be as easy as a quick handwritten thank you note (people are always amazed when they get a handwritten note) or a public acknowledgment of an individual or group for a job well done. Formal rewards are probably built into your performance management system, but consider sending one of your hardworking staff members home early one day or providing them with a small gift card for dinner with their spouse.

b. **Look for the good in the bad.** Although we don't want failure, it will happen. Analyzing what went wrong and then looking for the good in that situation will help relieve the pressures. Sometimes referred to as "reframing," this exercise provides alternative ways of seeing a particular situation. The classic example of this situation is when the best salesman gets promoted to sales manager and fails miserably. Some companies might consider firing him without realizing that his skills do not lay in managing but in selling.

c. **Maximize employee use of their benefits.** Insist that your employees use the benefits and perks of their job. Make sure they take their full vacation, and alert them to the availability of health care and family resources that can help with their children and their parents. Financial pressures are a major source of employee concerns, and services from retirement planning, bank loans, and educational financial assistance can help mitigate concerns on their part. Invite these resources to come to your company or workgroup once or twice a year to make sure that everyone is on board regarding these programs.

I am talking to more and more managers and leaders who want to take charge of their workplace and create a workspace where employees can do their greatest good and contribute to the success of their organization.

CHAPTER 10

End-to-End Resilience

We end the book in the same way we started, by pointing out that resilience is all around us and we want to connect with the larger efforts to build resilience. Giving up the idea that we can manage stress also means that we are no longer victimized by stress. Changing our behaviors to develop a new set of skills away from this model will take time and require small steps and a community of people to support the changes both at home and at work. Finding your resilience place will mean that every day is a new opportunity to find a successful path to meet and overcome, with grace and ease, the challenges of adversity.

A Resilience Story

I was on the tarmac at Dallas Fort Worth Airport (DFW) on September 11, 2001 at around 8:15 a.m. CDT, getting ready to head off to a business meeting, when the pilot announced we were having mechanical problems and he was going to head back to the terminal. Since most of us had heard only about the first plane that had hit the Trade Center North Tower, we were not aware of the second plane having hit the South Tower. Terrorism had struck our shores and our pilot, wanting to protect his plane, refrained from giving us the full message just in case our plane had also been targeted for terrorism. No one knew much of anything that morning.

Later, at my office, as our team huddled around the TV watching the events of the day play out, I received a phone call from American Airlines, which was headquartered at DFW Airport. Having consulted with them for a number of years and having experience in dealing with traumatic events, they asked if we could send a few of our clinical and organizational consulting staff over to the airport to provide support to their employees. They did not know how long they would need us.

The next day, several colleagues and I drove out to DFW and spent our first day and night meeting with staff at their call center. More than any of us, American Airlines employees were in extreme shock, having lost two planes that day, in New York and Washington. The call center staff was courageous in handling calls ranging from inquiries as sensitive as the names of lost family members to working to assist stranded travelers find a way home. Our job was to listen, lend support, help them talk through their emotions and thoughts, and begin, in whatever small way we could, a healing process.

Over the next several months, our team would spend countless hours at the airport meeting with employees at all levels of the organization, from senior executives at the corporate office to pilots, flight attendants, ramp personnel, and terminal employees.

But just a week or so after 9/11, I was walking down Terminal A at the DFW airport. While flights had resumed, there were few if any travelers, and the terminals resembled ghost towns more than the transportation hubs they were intended to be. That day, my job was to walk the terminal to talk to any employees who might want to talk. From one corner of a seating area, I saw a flight attendant being comforted by a colleague.

As I approached, I could see that she was crying. She could not seem to catch her breath as her tears streamed down her face. I went over and introduced myself, explaining that I was an organizational psychologist and had been asked by American Airlines to make myself available to staff here at the terminal or anywhere in the corporate offices. I asked whether I could be of assistance to her and she invited me to sit down. Her colleague was glad the cavalry had arrived and was relieved to scamper off to her assignment. The flight attendant, Susan, had a story like others I had heard over the previous week. She was in the air when the order to land was issued and, without knowing the full story of what had happened to her fellow colleagues, moved into her professional mode of operation ensuring that passengers were all safe and that the plane successfully returned to the ground.

She took care of her paperwork, connected with colleagues to make sure they were safe, and alerted her family that all was okay. She managed to get back to her home in Dallas after a few days and today represented her first flight back since 9/11. Although her week had been incredibly difficult, she had managed to keep herself together, reaching out to friends and colleagues and talking about the sheer magnitude of the events that had transpired. She felt like she was doing as well as she could until she arrived at the airport that morning for her afternoon flight when the events just hit her like a pile of bricks.

Over the next several hours, I just sat and listened to her. She told me of the friend she lost on one of the flights and how she could not imagine getting back on a plane again and flying. Her emotions ebbed and flowed during our time together. One moment she would be in disbelief that all of this happened. The next she would be in tears. Soon she might be angry about it. All of it was leading her to one conclusion that she would not be able to fly that day.

She soon told me about her history at American Airlines. She was a 20-year employee, deeply committed to the company and her profession. She saw herself as more than a flight attendant. She believed that her job was to help bring people together. She loved flying, and was gratified that she had been able to fly around the world.

I could see that she was beginning to tap into her professional roots. She had started her career excited for the adventures that awaited her, but now as a seasoned professional, she understood the pluses and minuses. She had seen the best and now she was living the worst.

It was at this point in our conversation that I saw a shift in her thinking. It wasn't so much that she was getting angry, but more that she was becoming resolute. It was as if a switch had been flipped and Susan saw that she had to get up and do this flight.

Soon she was wiping her final tears away and telling me that she had an obligation to fly that day. "I see that I have to fly today," she told me. "It may not feel like I'm ready to do it, but I just have to pick myself up and get on that plane. I know now that I have to do this for myself, my profession, my airline, my fallen colleagues, and for our country." And with that, Susan got up, thanked me with a hug, and headed off to her flight.

I spent the rest of the day in Terminal A wondering about the capacity that Susan had that allowed her to make that shift in just a matter of hours. It was then that I first saw the power of resilience.

It took several weeks before there were passengers and employees walking end-to-end in Terminal A. It took all of us a period of time to recognize that we had to adapt to a new way of traveling, to grieve those lost, and to rebuild from that day. But like the Freedom Tower that now stands in lower Manhattan, there was never a question that it would happen. We are resilient.

Your Resilience Strategy

It seems funny at one level that when it comes to big things that happen like 9/11, Hurricanes Katrina and Sandy, firestorms in the west, oil spills in the Gulf, and other natural and even man-made disasters, there is no question of our ability to respond effectively and quickly. In those cases, we jump to each other's aid, mobilize the resources that are necessary, and never question what we have to do. When it comes to dealing with our smaller personal and business challenges, however, we are never certain that we can overcome these seemingly smaller adversities. Somehow, in these situations, we become victims of our circumstances, unsure of what actions to take or whether the stress of the moment is too much for us to bear.

What we've tried to say in this book is that the stress management model, which has been our societal approach to addressing personal and organizational challenges, has actually limited our ability to marshal the forces we need to address the challenges of our day. By forcing us to think that all we can do is to try to hold on during the storm of stress, we've created a victimization model that doesn't work effectively and leaves us feeling bad about how we are incapable of dealing with almost any normal life event.

Instead, we can acknowledge and own the fact that resilience is a more natural way to address stress, and that resilience is hard wired into our system. Furthermore, these life's challenges are actually good for us in that they help us grow and learn.

Building an end-to-end approach to stress resilience means that you begin to see the benefits of a resilience approach and start to build it into your daily fabric of living. For some people, change in their life can be dramatic—seemingly and perhaps actually overnight. Unfortunately, that kind of change is usually accompanied by some kind of intense life-altering event, like a heart attack or car accident. When you see your life pass in front of you in swift visuals, it probably means you are going to be making some changes.

For the majority of us, however, the commitment to make a lifestyle change requires incremental steps. We look for small opportunities to implement an improvement, whether it's adding an extra day for workout, asking for a salad rather than French fries at lunch, or seeing how we can deal with our daily pressures in a way in which they do not overwhelm us.

Equally important to incrementality for seeking improvement is intentionality. Making a decision that we can do things differently sets the stage for new opportunities and experiences. Even if we do it "wrong," it becomes okay, since we are only experimenting and trying something new.

Manifesting resilience is not a big leap of faith or action. After all, resilience and not management is the natural order of how we respond to stress so in some ways. All we have to do is get out of the way of being resilient to be more resilient. Yet, developing a little plan can be helpful in moving us along toward having a more resilient lifestyle:

- **Pay attention to what you say to yourself.** Our inner voice drives a significant part of how we live our lives. And most of the time, our inner voice is telling us that we're not that good or able to deal with the challenge we are facing. If you discover that your self-messages are usually self-limiting, then consider undertaking the physical activity of writing a new set of messages that you can keep on your computer screen or in your office that resets the old messages.
- **Ask the right questions.** Many of us begin questioning ourselves by asking "why" we did something or "why" something happened. *Why* questions can be helpful in understanding events and their origins, but I've always been more interested in *how* questions. How did I do? Or how can I do things better. Exploring the how part of your actions will lead to better actions that create more of a resilience reaction rather than a management action.

- **Model the best.** Who are your avatars, the people to whom you look up and who seem to do well in most situations? Sure, if you talk with them, they'll probably tell you that they have more than their share of difficulties in navigating life's adversities. You can bet that they will also tell you that they've developed some tried and true strategies that work for them and that you can probably try out as well.

- **Watch your language.** What we speak externally is just as powerful as what we say to ourselves internally. Recently, I was at a convenience store getting a breakfast sandwich. When the woman behind the counter called my number, she also told me to "make it a good day." Usually what you hear from people is "have a good day," but when she told me to "make it a good day," I realized that the success of my day is in my hands and that only I can ensure that I have a winning day.

- **Set your vision.** Imagine how much easier your life will be when you stop beating yourself up for mistakes that you make and instead look at those events as learning opportunities. Or how much more quickly you'll be able to recover from tough days when you've reworked your schedule, so that you finish all you have to do at work and don't bring home an additional three hours of work. Creating visual pictures and images of how you'll be more resilient will help shape that reality.

- **Show your gratitude.** On our website you will find a downloadable Gratitude Journal: a 28-day journal that will help you track your appreciation and learnings on an everyday basis, and will help you see the successes that you bring to the world every day.

- **Share the energy.** As you manifest more resilience, you'll be shocked to see how much energy and ineffectiveness others demonstrate in how they address their stress. Small ideas can have a big impact on how you help others see another path from managing their life challenges. A colleague of mine, Soyinka Rahim, has coined the term "BIBO," pronounced

"Bee-Bow" (as in bow and arrow), which means "Breathe In, Breathe Out." For Soyinka and her students, whenever they get into a tough place, they use this expression to remind themselves of the importance of breathing as a way of finding a quiet and easy place to deal with that event.

- **Create rituals.** Changing behaviors is always challenging. We often tell ourselves we have to stop doing something like smoking or losing weight and then find that we are not successful and bemoan ourselves for having poor self-control. A better approach to change is through substitution for unwanted behaviors. Instead of stopping something, try doing something else instead. Creating a ritual or daily routine that you engage in every day helps to create an easy discipline. For example, if you want to begin exercising more, put a note on your desk that says, "Take the stairs." Need a better e-mail strategy? Make a note to check e-mail at specified times each day. Regarding food, I suggest that you make better bad choices. Feeling like French fries tonight? Go ahead and order them as an appetizer and share them with your party.

- **Protect the plan.** There will always be a counter weight pulling you back toward trying to manage stress. It will in part be related to your learned behaviors over the course of your lifetime, along with the many messages we get in the media and from others that we are incapable of shaping how life events unravel. Maintaining your resilient mindset will, for a period of time, require you to keep reminding yourself to practice the skills of resilience. Over time, we can reach a tipping point where thinking and being resilient works better for us than just trying to manage through our life.

You will find more ideas and forms you can use to create your personal stress resilience strategy at our website, **www.resilienceadvantage.com**. Use the password **resilienceadvantage** to access materials.

A Resilient Future

The common view on resilience focuses on bounce back, but as I saw in the face of Susan, the flight attendant, resilience can be so much more. We return to our definition of resilience—

Resilience is our ability to effectively plan for, navigate successfully in real time, and gracefully recover from challenging and stressful events in such a way that we are strengthened by the experience.

We are reading or hearing about resilience almost every day. News commentators talk about resilient communities overcoming everything from floods to fires. Sports announcers detail athletes and teams that overcome injuries and losses to find victory on the field. Former rust belt cities like Cleveland and Pittsburgh consider themselves models of resilience.

Common usage of the word often depicts challenges associated with big and traumatic events that create societal chaos, yet the day-to-day trials that we refer to as our stressful life are perfect opportunities to think, "I am resilient." Resilience as a personal strategy for our workplace and homelife is just beginning to find its footing, as we move from an understanding of the idea to putting it into play.

With actions like the Rockefeller's grant funding for chief resilience officers across 100 global cities, resilience is going to become a centerpiece for planning and management of how communities can build safer infrastructures, address crises more effectively when they occur, and build plans to make sure that when bad things happen, the community has a plan for recovery. However, having these models in place won't work unless they are sustainable. At some point, the grant funds will turn off. Unless community partners have created a belief in the value of resilience as a way of coping with the world, the project will merely fall off the map and will be another series of loose-leaf binders collecting dust in some county office.

It is, in part, for this reason why the development of personal and organizational resilience is so critical to the overall success of transforming our old and flawed models of stress management into something new. If we work from the top down in building a societal approach to adversity and from the bottom-up in building personal resilience, at some point we will meet in the middle in our social institutions, which are our workplaces, our churches, synagogues, and mosques, and in our families.

The good news, of course, is that resilience is built into us. It is our natural tendency to want to come back stronger, so in this regard, our capacity for resilience is omnipresent. Yet we must still learn how to effectively create resilient behaviors—optimism, agility, asking for help, using strengths, learning from failure while at the same time putting aside the flawed message that we are incapable of dealing effectively with stress.

Each of us also has unique qualities, strengths, and weaknesses that will work best for building resilience. There is no magic bullet that will make our stress go away. Everyone's formula will be a bit different. But when we see that our challenges and adversities actually help us grow and become the people and organizations we aspire to become, we'll have completed the transition from managing stress to becoming masterfully resilient.

References

American Psychological Association. (2014). *Stress in America: Paying With Our Health.* Accessed online at http://www.apa.org/news/press/releases/stress/index.aspx?tab=1

Berg, J.M., Dutton, J.E. & Wrzisniewski, A. (2010). *Job Crafting Exercise.* Center for Positive Organizations, University of Michigan, Ann Arbor, MI.

Cabot-Zinn. (2012). *Mindfulness for Beginners.* Sounds True, Inc. Boulder, CO.

Collins, S. (2013). *Warrior Mother: A Memoir of Fierce Love, Unbearable Loss and Rituals that Heal.* She Writes Press. Berkeley, CA.

Duckworth, A. (2007). Grit: Perseverance and Passion for Long-Term Goals. *Journal of Personality and Social Psychology, 92(6):* 1087–1101.

Dweck, C. (2006). *Mindset: the New Psychology of Success.* Ballantine Books, New York.

Forrester Research. (2014). *The State of Business Technology Resiliency.* Accessed online at http://ibm.co/1R2W7Gi

Fredrickson, B. (2009). *Positivity: To-Notch Research Reveals the 3 to 1 Ratio That Will Change Your Life.* Three Rivers Press. New York.

Gallup Organization. (2014). *Majority of US Employees Not Engaged Despite Gains in 2014.* Accessed online at http://bit.ly/1uUCjpX

Gehler, C.P. (2014). *Agile Leaders, Agile Institutions: Educating Adaptive and Innovative Leaders for Today and Tomorrow.* US Army War College. Accessed online at http://1.usa.gov/1VN8BRC

Glassdoor Blog. (2014). *Average US Employee Only Takes Half of Earned Vacation Time: Glassdoor Employment Confidence Survey.* Accessed online at http://bit.ly/1SHv4QE

Grant. A. (2010). *Putting a Face to a Name: The Art of Motivating Employees.* Knowledge@Work, Wharton School of Business, University of Pennsylvania, Philadelphia, PA.

Hollander, J. (March, 2010). *How I Did It: Giving Up the CEO Seat.* Harvard Business Review.

Ito, T.A., Larsen, J.T. Smith, N.K. & Cacioppo, J.T. (1998). Negative Information Weighs More Heavily on the Brain: The Negativity Bias in Evaluative Categorizations. *Journal of Personality and Social Psychology, 75(4).*

Kantor, J. & Streitreld, D. (2015). *Inside Amazon: Wrestling Big Ideas in a Bruising Workplace.* New York Times. Accessed online at http://nyti.ms/1HNMWQq

Keller, A., Litzelman, K., Wisk, L. E., Maddox, T., Cheng, E. R., Creswell, P. D., & Witt, W. P. (2011, December 26). Does the Perception That Stress Affects

Health Matter? The Association With Health and Mortality. *Health Psychology 2012 Sep, 31(5):*677–84.

Lazarus, R. S., & Folkman, S. (1984). *Stress, appraisal, and coping.* Springer Publishing Company, New York.

Leonhardt, D. (1999). *More Bosses Encourage Napping on Job.* New York Times. Accessed online at http://nyti.ms/1R5gF0K.

Lombardo, M.W. & Eichinger, R.W. (2011). *The Leadership Machine: Architecture to Develop Leaders in Any Future.* Lominger International. Minneapolis, MN.

Maddi, S. & Khoshaba, D. (2005). *Resilience at Work.* AMACOM, New York.

Maslow, A. (1949). *A Theory of Human Motivation.* Psychological Review.

Oettingen, G. (2014). *Rethinking Positive Thinking: Inside the New Science of Motivation.* Current Publishers, New York.

Rendon, J. *Post Traumatic Stress's Surprisingly Positive Flip Side.* New York Times. Accessed online at http://nyti.ms/1Tw1kbY

Rosin, H. (April, 2014). *The Overprotected Kid.* The Atlantic. Accessed online at http://theatln.tc/1LrKFkI

Russell, B. & Branch, T. (1980). *Second Wind.* Ballentine Books, New York.

Schwartz. B. (August 28, 2015). *Rethinking Work.* New York Times Sunday Review. Accessed online at http://nyti.ms/1SK1LwQ

Sheffi, Y. (2005). *The Resilient Enterprise.* MIT Press. Boston, MA.

Shorto, R. (2014). *How to Think Like the Dutch in a Post-Sandy World.* New York Times. Accessed online at http://nyti.ms/1hgvDiM

Siegel, D. (2010). *PsychAlive.* Accessed online at http://bit.ly/1UFkw5Z

Southwick, S. & Charney, D. (2012). *Resilience: The Science of Mastering Life's Greatest Challenges.* Cambridge University Press, New York.

Southwick, S. (2012). *The Science of Resilience.* Accessed online at http://huff.to/1X5gCmb

Sullivan, P. (2010). *Clutch: Excel Under Pressure.* Portfolio, New York.

Swisher, V.V. (2012). *Becoming an Agile Leader.* Lominger International. Minneapolis, MN.

NOTES

Chapter 1

i. Rosin, H. *The Overprotected Kid*. The Atlantic. April 2014. http://bit.ly/209LYrW

ii. Rosin, ibid.

iii. Dan Gilbert. *The surprising science of happiness*. http://bit.ly/1lS8Y1l

iv. Gilbert, ibid.

Chapter 2

v. Lily Tomlin quote. http://bit.ly/1oVvIiy

vi. Gallup. Gallup Organization. *Majority of US Employees Not Engaged Despite Gains in 2014*. http://bit.ly/1TE9hdy

vii. Glassdoor. *Average US Employee Only Takes Half of Earned Vacation Time: Glassdoor Employment Confidence Survey*. 2014. http://bit.ly/1SHv4QE

viii. American Psychological Association. *Stress in America: Paying With Our Health*. http://apa.org/news/press/releases/stress/2014/stress-report.pdf

ix. American Psychological Association, ibid.

x. American Psychological Association, ibid.

xi. Yerkes Dodson Law. National Institutes of Health. http://1.usa.gov/1TEc4Dz

xii. Yerkes Dodson curve. National Institutes of Health. http://1.usa.gov/1TEc4Dz

xiii. Roald Amundsen. Wikipedia. https://en.wikipedia.org/wiki/Roald_Amundsen

xiv. Werner, E., Bierman, J.M., & French, F.E. *The Children of Kauai: A Longitudinal Study from the Prenatal Period to Age Ten*. University of Hawaii Press. Honolulu, Hawaii. 1971.

xv. Werner, E. & Smith, R.S. *Vulnerable but Invincible: A Longitudinal Study of Resilient Children and Youth*. Adams Bannister Cox. New York. 1982.

xvi. Werner, E. Resilience and Recovery: Finding from the Kauai Longitudinal Study. *Focal Point* Summer, 2005 Vol. 19 No.1, pp. 11–14. Portland State University.

xvii. Southwick, S. & Charney, D. *Resilience: The Science of Mastering Life's Greatest Challenges*. Cambridge University Press. New York. 2012.

xviii.   Southwick, S., & Charney, D. ibid.

xix.   Mayor Nagin. Timeline of Hurricane Katrina. Wikipedia
https://en.wikipedia.org/wiki/Timeline_of_Hurricane_Katrina

xx.   Governor Chris Christi. Hurricane Sandy.
https://en.wikipedia.org/wiki/Hurricane_Sandy

xxi.   Implementing 9/11 Commission Recommendations. Progress Report,
2011. http://1.usa.gov/1X3QSqn

xxii.   A year after Sandy, new initiative aims to help "resilient" cities prepare for
disaster. Forbes Magazine, 2013 http://onforb.es/1SYq5g0

xxiii.   Forbes Magazine, ibid.

xxiv.   Warren Buffet is my boss and it's a happy marriage: BNSF's Rose. CNBC
interview http://cnb.cx/1QGyi4X

xxv.   Oil tank car fire forces evacuation of North Dakota Town. New York
Times. http://nyti.ms/1IS8j7W

xxvi.   The state of business technology resiliency Q2, 2014. Forrester Research.
http://ibm.co/1R2W7Gi

Chapter 3

xxvii.   Russell, B., & Branch, T. *Second Wind*. Ballantine, Books. New York. 1980.

xxviii.   Lazarus, R.S., & Folkman, S. *Stress, appraisal, and coping*. New York, NY:
Springer Publishing Company. 1984.

xxix.   Lazarus, R.S., & Folkman, S. ibid.

xxx.   http://www.gallup.com/poll/181289/majority-employees-not-engaged-
despite-gains-2014.aspx

xxxi.   Taleb, N.N. *The Black Swan: The Impact of Highly Improbable*. Random
House. New York. 2007.

xxxii.   Diane Lane. http://www.brainyquote.com/quotes/authors/d/diane_lane.html

Chapter 4

xxxiii.   Sullivan, P. *Clutch: Excel Under Pressure*. Portfolio. New York. 2010.

xxxiv.   *Ballmer laughs at iPhone*. Youtube.
https://www.youtube.com/watch?v=eywi0h_Y5_U

xxxv.   Margaret Thatcher quote. Heartquote. http://heartquotes.com/Expert.html

xxxvi.   Tetlock, P.E. *Expert Political Judgment: How Good is it? How Can We
Know?* Princeton University Press. Princeton, NJ. 2005.

xxxvii.   Tetlock, ibid.

xxxviii.   Switzer. K. *Marathon Woman: Running the Race to Revolutionize Women's
Sports*. Carrol and Graf, New York. 2007.

xxxix. Duckworth, A. Grit: Perseverance and Passion for Long-Term Goals *Journal of Personality and Social Psychology, 2007 V.92, No. 6 1087–1101.*

xl.   Woody Allen.
      http://www.brainyquote.com/quotes/quotes/w/woodyallen145883.html

xli. Duckworth, ibid.

xlii. Keller, A., Litzelman, K., Wisk, L. E., Maddox, T., Cheng, E. R., Creswell, P. D., & Witt, W. P. (2011, December 26). Does the Perception That Stress Affects Health Matter? The Association With Health and Mortality. *Health Psychology* 2012 Sep; 31(5):677–84.

xliii. Dweck, C. *Mindset: the New Psychology of Success.* Ballantine Books. New York. 2006.

xliv. Dweck, ibid.

Chapter 5

xlv.   Siegel, D. *Psych Alive.* Minding The Brain. 2010. http://bit.ly/1q04RRG

xlvi. Siegel, D. http://www.drdansiegel.com/about/interpersonal_neurobiology/

xlvii. Simmons, R. *Success Through Stillness.* Gotham Books. 2014. New York

xlviii. Brandi, C. http://usat.ly/1rsMq2X

xlix. Jeff, H. *How I Did It: Giving up the CEO Seat.* http://bit.ly/1KqHg6Y

Chapter 6

l.   Sheffi, Y. *The Resilient Enterprise.* MIT Press. Boston, MA. 2005.

li.   Taleb, N.N. *The Black Swan: The Impact of Highly Improbable.* Random House. New York. 2007.

lii.   Taleb, N.N. *Antifragile: Things that Gain from Disorder.* Random House. New York. 2012.

liii.   Collins, S. *Warrior Mother: A Memoir of Fierce Love, Unbearable Loss and Rituals that Heal.* She Writes Press. Berkeley, CA. 2013.

liv.   Collins, ibid.

Chapter 7

lv.   Maslow, A. A Theory of Human Motivation. *Psychological Review.* 1949.

lvi.   Ito, T.A., Larsen, J.T., Smith, N.K., & Cacioppo, J.T. Negative Information Weighs More Heavily on the Brain: the Negativity Bias in Evaluative Categorizations. *Journal of Personality and Social Psychology.* 1998. Vol. 75. No 4.

lvii.   Akhwari, J. https://en.wikipedia.org/wiki/John_Stephen_Akhwari

lviii.   Weiss, A. *Million Dollar Maverick*. Bibliomotion, New York, 2016.

lix.   http://www.brainyquote.com/quotes/quotes/t/thomasjeff121032.html

lx.   Weisand, M. *Rewiring Your Brain Ted Talk*. http://usat.ly/1rsMq2X

lxi.   Oettingen, G. *Rethinking Positive Thinking: Inside the New Science of Motivation*. Current Publishers. New York. 2014.

lxii.   Oettingen ibid

Chapter 8

lxiii.   Dweck, C. *Mindset: the New Psychology of Success*. Ballantine Books. New York. 2006.

lxiv.   Forest Gump, Paramount Pictures, 1994.

lxv.   Rendon, J. *Post-Traumatic Stress's Surprisingly Positive Flip Side*. New York Times. 2012. http://nyti.ms/1S0PC7S

lxvi.   Dweck, C. *Mindset: the New Psychology of Success*. Ballantine Books. New York. 2006.

lxvii.   Thomas Edison. http://bit.ly/1VMVYGl

lxviii. Winston Churchill. http://bit.ly/1P7bwms

lxix.   http://bit.ly/1uUCjpX

lxx.   Maddi, S. & Khoshaba, D. *Resilience at Work*. AMACOM. New York. 2005.

Chapter 9

lxxi   Inside Amazon: Wrestling Big Ideas in a Bruising Workplace. 2015. http://nyti.ms/1HNMWQq

lxxii.   Mike Tyson. http://bit.ly/209JMkb

lxxiii. Glassdoor. *Average US Employee Only Takes Half of Earned Vacation Time: Glassdoor Employment Confidence Survey*. 2014. http://bit.ly/1SHv4QE

lxxiv.   Swisher, V.V. *Becoming an Agile Leader*. Lominger International. Minneapolis. 2012.

lxxv.   Gehler, C.P. *Agile Leaders, Agile Institutions,* US Army War College. 2014. http://1.usa.gov/1VN8BRC

lxxvi.   Target data breach. http://huff.to/1VNam1c

lxxvii. Anthem date breach. http://on.wsj.com/1zmrZN5

lxxviii. The Patriot. Columbia Pictures.

lxxix.   Berg, J.M., Dutton, J.E., & Wrzisniewski, A. *Job Crafting Exercise*. Center for Positive Organizations. University of Michigan. 2010.

lxxx. Adam Grant How Customers Can Rally Your Troops. *Harvard Business Review*. 2011. http://bit.ly/1StEEbP

lxxxi. Schwartz, B. *Rethinking Work*. New York Times. 2015. http://nyti.ms/1VNc3f5

lxxxii. Fredrickson, B. *Positivity: Top-Notch Research Reveals the 3 to 1 Ratio That Will Change Your Life*. Three Rivers Press. New York. 2009.

Index

.

.

CPSIA information can be obtained
at www.ICGtesting.com
Printed in the USA
BVOW09s0516281017
498906BV00004B/7/P